Renewable ENERGY

Discover the Fuel of the Future
with 20 PROJECTS

Joshua Sneideman
and Erin Twamley

Illustrated by
Heather Jane Brinesh

~ Recent Science Titles in the *Build It Yourself* Series ~

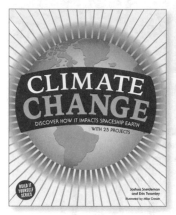

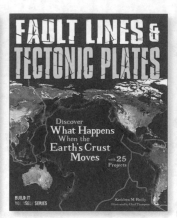
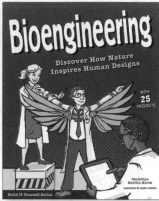

Check out more titles at www.nomadpress.net

Nomad Press
A division of Nomad Communications
10 9 8 7 6 5 4 3 2 1

This book was manufactured by Marquis Book Printing,
Montmagny Québec, Canada
April 2016, Job #121610

ISBN Softcover: 978-1-61930-360-7
ISBN Hardcover: 978-1-61930-356-0

Educational Consultant, Marla Conn

Questions regarding the ordering of this book should be addressed to
Nomad Press
2456 Christian St.
White River Junction, VT 05001
www.nomadpress.net

Printed in Canada.

National Energy
Education Development

The authors would like to thank
NEED for generously allowing
the use of their activities.

CONTENTS

Interested in Primary Sources?

Look for this icon. Use a smartphone or tablet app to scan the QR code and explore more about renewable energy! You can find a list of URLs on the Resources page.

If the QR code doesn't work, try searching the Internet with the Keyword Prompts to find other helpful sources.

renewable energy 🔍

2007: The Green Jobs Act is implemented.

1950s: Solar water heaters are used abundantly in Florida.

1830: In Hot Springs, Arkansas, Asa Thompson begins the first commercial use of geothermal energy for the use of three spring-fed baths.

2011: Total energy use per person in the United States is about 313 million British thermal units (Btu) compared to the world per person use of 75 million Btu.

1959: The world population reaches 3 billion people.

1881: Coal-fired steam-powered railway trains become the worldwide standard for passenger travel.

2000 BCE: The Chinese use coal as an energy source.

600 BCE: Thales, a Greek, discovers static electricity after rubbing amber and silk and noting the electric charge and attraction of objects.

1882: The world's first hydroelectric power plant begins operating in Wisconsin.

1970: The Geothermal Resources Council is formed as an international association for the geothermal energy industry.

200 BCE: One of the first windmills is invented in Persia, which is in present-day Iran.

2011: The world population reaches 7 billion people.

1892: Boise, Idaho, is powered by the United States' first geothermal energy heating system.

1600 CE: William Gilbert of England first coins the term electricity from *elektron*, the Greek word for amber.

2014: Solar energy systems are located on more than 3,700 K–12 schools in the United States.

1977: The U.S. Department of Energy is created as a new federal government agency.

1893: The first biofuel car engine is created.

1821: The first natural gas well in the United States is drilled.

1948: The Dover Sun House, in Massachusetts is the first occupied solar-powered house in the United States.

1982: Coal-generated electricity accounts for half the electricity used in the United States, but most is used for commercial purposes.

2015: The U.S. Clean Power Plan imposes the first nationwide limits on carbon dioxide emissions from power plants.

1805: The world population reaches 1 billion people.

1935: The Hoover Dam, the world's largest hydroelectric power plant, is built on the Arizona-Nevada border.

1981: The Renewables Fuel Association is formed in the United States.

1800: The residential sector consumes most of America's energy.

1930: More than half of Americans live in cities heated by coal.

2014: Ivanpah, the world's largest concentrated solar power generation plant, goes online.

1767: The first attempt to use a solar cooker to cook food is recorded.

1980: The world's first wind farm is opened in New Hampshire.

1748: Commercial coal production begins in Richmond, Virginia.

1908: Henry Ford produces the Model T car that can run on gasoline, ethanol, or any combination of the two.

2014: Renewable sources of energy account for about 10 percent of total U.S. energy consumption and 13 percent of electricity generation.

1900: Gasoline and ethanol begin competing for use in cars.

1979: The first solar panels are installed on the White House.

v

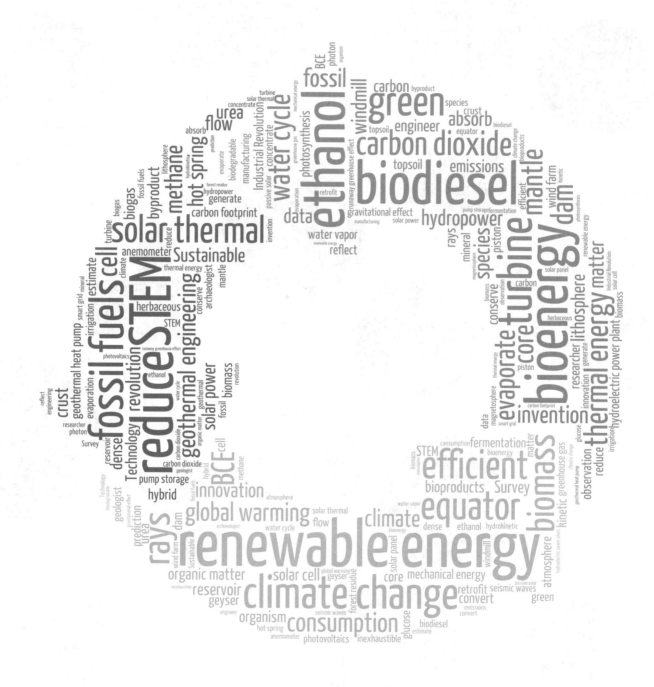

OPENING CEREMONIES

Look around you. Are your lights on? Is your computer running? We use energy every day to power our world. Most of the energy we use comes from fossil fuels, but renewable energy is another option.

In this book, we'll investigate five different renewable energies. Each of the five interconnected Olympic circles represents a renewable energy: yellow for the sun, black for wind, blue for water, green for biomass, and red for geothermal. You will discover how these forms work separately and together to produce clean energy.

WORDS TO KNOW

renewable energy: a form of energy that doesn't get used up, including the energy of the sun and the wind.

biomass: plant materials and animal waste used as fuel.

geothermal: heat energy from beneath the earth's surface.

1

innovation: a new invention or way of doing something.

technology: tools, methods, and systems used to solve a problem or do work.

engineering: the use of science and math in the design and construction of things.

fossil fuels: coal, oil, and natural gas. These energy sources come from the fossils of plants and tiny animals that lived millions of years ago.

global warming: an increase in the earth's average temperatures, enough to change the climate.

BCE: put after a date, BCE stands for Before Common Era and counts down to zero. CE stands for Common Era and counts up from zero. The year this book is published is 2016 CE.

solar power: energy from the sun converted to electricity.

Industrial Revolution: a period of time beginning in the late 1700s when people started using machines to make things in large factories.

WORDS TO KNOW

These renewable energy technologies are striving for a single shared goal—a cleaner future.

This book highlights the passion, hard work, and innovation of people working in the fields of science, technology, and engineering. Renewable energy is competing against fossil fuels, which have dominated the energy industry for the past 150 years. Fossil fuels cause air and water pollution and contribute to global warming. Using renewable energies will help create a cleaner planet.

A History of Renewable Energy

The use of renewable energy dates back thousands of years. Humans have been looking to the world around them for energy answers for a long time.

Wind was used as early as about 5000 BCE as a power source to propel boats along the Nile River in Egypt. Sometime around 3,000 years ago, the Persians began using wind power to pump water and grind grain.

Humans have also been harnessing water to perform work for thousands of years. The Greeks used water wheels for grinding wheat into flour more than 2,000 years ago.

Solar power is not new, either. Its history spans nearly 3,000 years, from the seventh century BCE to today. We started out concentrating the sun's heat with glass and mirrors to light fires. Now we use solar panels to convert the sun into electricity.

The first known use of geothermal energy occurred more than 10,000 years ago in North America. People used water from hot springs for cooking, bathing, and cleaning.

Times change and people try new things. In the 1800s, the use of renewable power, which for centuries had been mankind's only source of power, became overwhelmed by the needs of the Industrial Revolution. At that point, our modern civilization and its rapid expansion became powered mostly by fossil fuels. We needed these fossil fuels to power factories and new forms of transportation, such as trains and planes. People didn't realize that there was a high price for using fossil fuel—climate change.

Now, renewable energies are experiencing a resurgence. In the past few decades, there have been major advances in the science and technology used to harness energy from different renewable energy sources.

The urgent need to slow global warming and climate change is pushing us to make breakthroughs in the field of renewable energy.

Fossil Fuels

Coal, oil, and natural gas are called fossil fuels because they come from animal and plant fossils. Our planet of more than 7 billion people runs on energy from fossil fuels. People burn fossil fuels to create the energy we need to drive cars, power computers, heat and cool homes, and refrigerate food. About 90 percent of the world's electricity comes from burning fossil fuels.

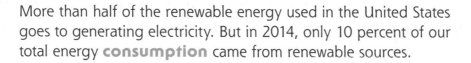

Plugged In

More than half of the renewable energy used in the United States goes to generating electricity. But in 2014, only 10 percent of our total energy **consumption** came from renewable sources.

Humans have been using fossil fuels since the 1700s. But burning fossil fuels harms the planet and human health by causing pollution and damaging our air, water, and **climate**.

Fossil fuels are found everywhere on the planet, from the oceans to deserts, from the Arctic to the tropics. The energy in those ancient plants and animals came from the sun. When we use this energy to cook our food, drive our cars, and make electricity, we are using solar energy and releasing stored **carbon** from millions of years ago.

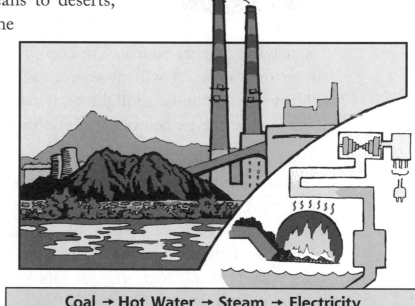

Coal → Hot Water → Steam → Electricity

When coal-fired power plants generate electricity, they release harmful **emissions** into the **atmosphere**. These include **greenhouse gases** such as **carbon dioxide** and **methane**, plus other harmful gasses that cause acid rain, smog, and health problems. Toxic metals such as mercury, lead, arsenic, and cadmium are also released, and are known to cause birth defects and other health problems.

5

WORDS TO KNOW

inexhaustible: impossible to use up completely.

green: something made from a renewable resource that does not harm the environment.

revolution: a human-led dramatic change in something.

sustainable: a process or resource that can be used without being completely used up or destroyed.

Power plants that use solar, wind, water, or geothermal energy to generate electricity do not release these harmful chemicals.

Choosing Renewables

Both the search for fossils fuels and the use of these energy sources hurts our planet. What if we could use electricity generated from renewable energy to light our homes and power our cars and electronics? It is possible.

Renewable energy sources are energy sources that do not pollute our air or water and will never get used up. Society will never run out of sunlight or wind. In fact, all renewable energy sources are **inexhaustible**.

Today, the future of our planet's climate is uncertain. The threat of global warming is very real. About 97 percent of scientists agree that burning fossil fuels is responsible for global warming and climate change. Renewable energy power plants can help us generate electricity without releasing harmful chemicals.

The sun will keep providing energy for millions of years. The wind is always going to blow. The ocean has regular tides, waves, and currents that, if captured, could help us power our lives. A new generation of scientist farmers can produce **green** liquid fuels from plants for our cars. Geothermal power, originating at the center of the earth, will last as long as our planet.

Moving from nonrenewable fossil fuels to renewable energy sources is critical if we are going to control global warming.

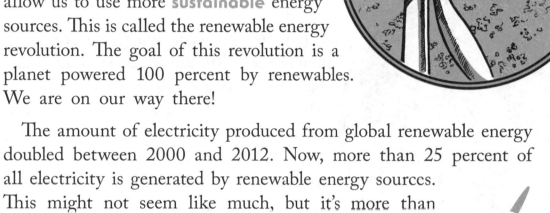

Right now, we are witnessing a **revolution** in how we generate and use energy. Rapid advances in technology allow us to use more **sustainable** energy sources. This is called the renewable energy revolution. The goal of this revolution is a planet powered 100 percent by renewables. We are on our way there!

The amount of electricity produced from global renewable energy doubled between 2000 and 2012. Now, more than 25 percent of all electricity is generated by renewable energy sources. This might not seem like much, but it's more than ever before and it's increasing.

Is Global Warming Real?

If greenhouse gases are naturally occurring, how do they cause global warming and climate change? The problem is that we are adding so much extra carbon dioxide (CO_2) to the environment so quickly that it is destroying the delicate balance of gases in the atmosphere and causing global temperatures to rise. Warmer temperatures lead to changing climates around the world.

There has been climate change in the past, but previous periods of climate change happened much more gradually than now. Most scientists agree that humans are raising the levels of CO_2 at a far higher rate than the most destructive periods of climate change in the earth's history.

scientific method:
the way scientists ask
questions and do
experiments to try to
prove their ideas.

trade-off: a compromise.

WORDS TO KNOW

Plugged In

Watch this animated TED-Ed video,
"A Guide to the Energy of the Earth."
Learn how energy is cycling through
our planet, from the sun to our food
chain to electricity.

TED-Ed guide energy earth 🔍

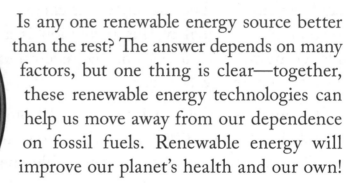

Is any one renewable energy source better
than the rest? The answer depends on many
factors, but one thing is clear—together,
these renewable energy technologies can
help us move away from our dependence
on fossil fuels. Renewable energy will
improve our planet's health and our own!

Our investigation into renewable energies
begins with a look at solar energy. Let's
explore the incredible energy from the sun that
has powered our planet for the past 4.5 billion years.

ENERGY TRADE-OFFS

All Energy Sources Have Pros and Cons

No energy source is 100 percent perfect. Each comes with its own
trade-offs and impacts on the environment. Trade-offs always need to
be compared between energy sources. As we learn about the different
sources of renewable energy, we'll examine these trade-offs and how
they impact us and our planet.

Good Science Practices

Every good scientist keeps a science journal! Scientists use the **scientific method** to keep their experiments organized. Choose a notebook to use as your science journal. As you read through this book and do the activities, keep track of your observations and record each step in a scientific method worksheet, like the one shown here.

Each chapter of this book begins with an essential question to help guide your exploration of renewable energy.

Keep the question in your mind as you read the chapter. At the end of each chapter, use your science journal to record your thoughts and answers.

Question: What are we trying to find out? What problem are we trying to solve?
Research: What do other people think?
Hypothesis/Prediction: What do we think the answer will be?
Equipment: What supplies are we using?
Method: What procedure are we following?
Results: What happened? Why?

ESSENTIAL QUESTION

Why is renewable energy considered a clean energy?

OILY FEATURES

IDEAS FOR SUPPLIES

science journal and pencil • *dry, clean feathers* • *magnifying glass* • *4 bowls* • *water* • *vegetable oil* • *cocoa powder* • *soap*

Imagine you are a bird and you've landed in the water with floating oil from an oil spill. What does it feel like on your feathers? How does it make you move differently? Investigate the impacts of an oil spill on animal life by testing bird feathers you find.

1 Observe your feathers. What do they look like? How do they feel? How do they help birds fly? Record your observations and analysis in your science journal and start a scientific method worksheet. Use a magnifying glass to examine the feathers more closely.

2 Fill a bowl halfway with room-temperature water.

3 Drop some feathers in the bowl and record what happens in your science journal. Include a hypothesis about what will happen to the water if you add oil to it. What will happen to the feathers if oil gets on them? Remove the feathers from the bowl and dry them.

Plugged In

What's a way that you can join the renewable energy revolution right now? Stop using plastic bags. Oil is used to make plastic bags and many of these bags end up in our oceans. Use reusable bags while shopping.

(PS) Oil Spills

Oil spills are a common consequence of our huge demand for oil. Oil spills have a negative impact on our environment that can last for many years. Some of the most devastating oil spills happen in the ocean. In 2010, an oil rig drilling for oil exploded in the Gulf of Mexico, spilling more than 210 million gallons of oil. The oil spill stretched across multiple states and countries. In 1969, an oil spill happened near Cape Cod, Massachusetts. Scientists still find evidence of oil in that area, nearly 50 years later. You can watch a video about one of the scientists working on this problem.

oil water don't mix ocean portal 🔍

4 In a separate bowl, mix together ½ cup vegetable oil with some cocoa powder. This will be the crude oil you might find after an oil spill.

5 Create an oil spill. Mix the oil into the large bowl with water. What happens? Record your observations.

6 Add the feathers to your oil spill. This is what a water bird experiences after an oil spill in the ocean. What happens to the feathers? What does it feel and look like? How would this affect a bird's ability to fly?

TRY THIS: Can you clean the feathers? Try three different methods—with just cold water, just hot water, and with soapy water. Create a table in your science journal to record the results. How is this information useful for helping animals after oil spills?

ACTIVITY

11

BURNING FOSSIL FUELS

IDEAS FOR SUPPLIES
Pyrex glass container • *candle* • *science journal and pencil*

Burning fossil fuels releases large amounts of carbon dioxide into the earth's atmosphere. Large quantities of carbon dioxide are linked to global climate change. Humans release on average annually about 64 trillion pounds of carbon dioxide into the atmosphere. That is like releasing 3.2 trillion watermelons into the sky every year. Since greenhouse gases are invisible, colorless, and odorless, we can't see the impact. Compare that with renewable energy sources such as wind, water, and solar, which release no gases into the air. Which do you think is better for our planet? Observe firsthand what burning a paraffin wax candle puts into the air. Paraffin wax is made from petroleum, which is a fossil fuel.

Caution: An adult must supervise the use of matches and a candle. Make sure to use a Pyrex glass container.

1 Fill the Pyrex container with ice and water. With the help of an adult, light the candle with your match.

2 Hold the glass cup of ice water directly above the flame for 2 to 3 seconds. Continue to hold the cup over the flame as you blow out the candle.

3 Observe the bottom of the cup. What do you notice about your candle emissions? What color is it and what does it look like? What happens when you touch it? What do you think it is? Record your observations in your science journal.

TRY THIS: Try the same experiment using a beeswax candle. Bees transform nectar from flowers into beeswax. Do you get the same result? What conclusions can you draw from comparing the two results?

Chapter 1

THE POWER OF THE SUN

Legend says that the Olympic torch was once lit with fire from the sun. While we can't actually get close enough to the sun to steal its fire, we can use energy from the sun in many different ways.

People have been using solar power since the beginning of human history, but it's only recently that we've developed the technologies we need to harness the energy of the sun. Scientists and engineers are now working to make these technologies more **efficient** and more useful every day.

? ESSENTIAL QUESTION

How can we use the sun to produce energy here on the earth?

efficient: wasting as little as possible.

data: facts about something that can be analyzed.

rays: lines of light that come from a bright object.

absorb: to soak up a liquid or take in energy, heat, light, or sound.

reflect: to redirect something that hits a surface, such as heat, light, or sound.

species: a group of living things that are closely related and can produce young.

solar panel: a device used to capture sunlight and convert it to usable energy.

STEM: stands for science, technology, engineering, and math. Add art for STEAM.

WORDS TO KNOW

Plugged In

In one day, the earth receives more energy from the sun than the world uses in one year! The sun will make energy for billions of years. We will never run out of it.

What is the sun? Most people think of the sun as a featureless, unchanging ball of light. The sun is actually the star at the center of our solar system. Without it, we wouldn't exist.

For centuries, people have studied the sun. Scientists at the National Aeronautics and Space Administration (NASA) have studied the sun with satellites that are capable of collecting lots of **data**. This data shows that the sun's energy is released in a regular pattern.

Solar energy comes to the earth in the form of **rays**. There are many types of rays, including radio, infrared, ultraviolet, X-ray, and gamma rays. The sun emits different kinds of rays, including ultraviolet, visible light, and infrared. Some of these rays are **absorbed** and some are **reflected** back into space by the earth's atmosphere. The rays that are absorbed help to warm our atmosphere and make it possible for different **species** to live here.

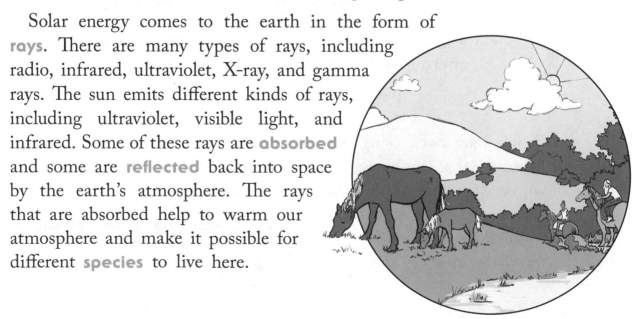

Solar Electricity

Humans have used solar energy throughout history. We know the sun's rays were used to help build fires as early as 700 BCE. A "heat ray" weapon used in 214–212 BCE concentrated the sun's energy using mirrors to burn sails on warring ships. But solar energy must be converted into electricity so that we can use it today. Energy cannot be created or destroyed, so how do we use solar energy?

Today, we convert solar energy into electricity that we use to power many things. These include devices in our homes and businesses and different means of transportation. One of the most common ways of turning solar energy into power is with **solar panels**.

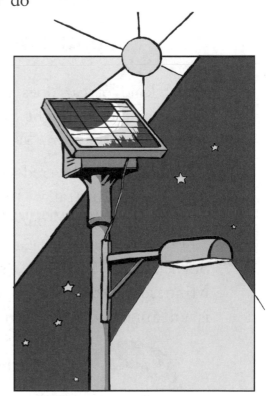

Look around your neighborhood. Do you see any solar panels? You might see them on the roofs of buildings or freestanding in fields or yards. Solar panels can power streetlights, parking garages, houses, businesses, calculators, and even radios.

Solar Jobs

Solar jobs are considered to be "clean" or "green" jobs. This term refers to jobs that help protect our environment and the earth. Solar jobs require knowledge and skills in science, technology, engineering, art, and math. You might have heard these subjects called the **STEM** or STEAM subjects. STEM jobs, especially in renewable energy, are fast growing and diverse.

engineer: a person who uses science, math, and creativity to design and build things.

generate: to create something or to produce energy.

WORDS TO KNOW

In Holland, **engineers** have designed a new solar bike path that **generates** enough solar-powered electricity to light the path and other areas in the neighborhood. Can you imagine if all our sidewalks, driveways, and roads were made out of solar panels? We would have enough electricity for everyone on Earth.

Solar-Powered Transportation

What kind of car does your family drive? It's probably a car that uses gasoline. It might be a car that uses electricity, or maybe it's a hybrid of the two. What about a solar-powered car?

Today, solar-powered car races are held in Europe, the United States, and Australia. The first race was in Switzerland in 1985. It was called the Tour de Sol. The World Solar Challenge is a 3,000-kilometer solar car race across Australia. In the last American Solar racecar challenge, solar-powered cars drove from Texas to Minnesota. At the Texas Motor Speedway, the Solar Car Challenge is an annual event. Even high school students are entering solar races. Maybe your neighborhood high school will join the race.

GREEN JOBS

Engineers

Engineers are people who design and build new products, such as solar bike paths. Engineers are problem solvers. A current challenge in creating solar panels is to design them so that they can hold the weight of humans, cars, and bikes without breaking. This would enable us to have solar roads! Check out the video on the opening of a solar bike path in the Netherlands.

Netherlands glow cycle path 🔍

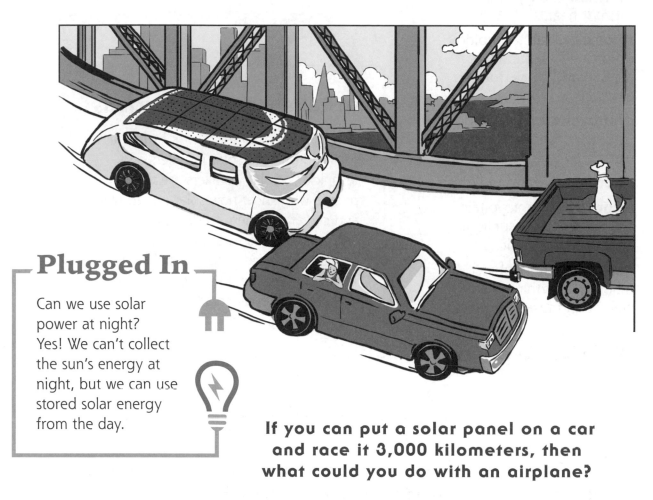

Plugged In

Can we use solar power at night? Yes! We can't collect the sun's energy at night, but we can use stored solar energy from the day.

If you can put a solar panel on a car and race it 3,000 kilometers, then what could you do with an airplane?

In August 2015, the first solar-powered plane flew around the world without using a single drop of fossil fuel. The flight of *Solar Impulse* included five days and nights of flying nonstop.

For decades, NASA has been using solar panels to power its missions, from satellites that orbit the earth to the International Space Station. Solar-powered space flight isn't new. NASA first used solar power in 1964 on a satellite called *Nimbus 1*. Aeronautical engineers began designing solar flight vehicles in the 1970s. Today, NASA is planning for human spaceflight to Mars with its *Orion* program. This mission is highly dependent on solar panels for success.

thermal: energy in the form of heat.

thermal: energy in the form of heat.

solar thermal: technology used to heat water from the sun and convert it into electricity.

photovoltaics: technology used to convert sunlight into electricity.

photon: a particle of light.

solar cell: a photovoltaic cell that converts sunlight directly into electricity.

matter: what an object is made of. Anything that has weight and takes up space.

WORDS TO KNOW

GREEN JOBS

Installers and Technicians

Two of the most important jobs in the solar industry are solar installers and technicians. Solar installers are the people who know how solar panels work and can attach them to roofs, airplanes, and cars. Businesses around the country specialize in solar installations. Technicians are people who can help monitor and repair solar systems once they are put in place.

Capturing the Sun

All of this solar energy is great, but how does it get from being the sun's rays to powering our cars and homes?

The sun would not be a useful renewable energy without our solar inventions. We can capture the energy using solar thermal technology or photovoltaics. There are two ways to generate electricity using photovoltaics. One method uses solar panels and the other uses reflective mirrors.

Sunlight is composed of photons. Photons are tiny particles of solar energy. It was Albert Einstein who helped us understand that light consists of photons. These photons contain a very specific amount of energy. A solar cell is the technology that can convert solar energy from a photon directly into electricity.

The first solar cells were created in 1954 at Bell Laboratories in New Jersey. Three scientists made these cells from silicon. Silicon is a common substance found in sand. It is used to make computer chips.

When traveling through empty space, all photons move at the speed of light, about 186,411 miles per second. One of the most important qualities of a photon is that it can collide with other **matter**. When photons strike a solar cell, they can be absorbed, passed through, or reflected. Photons whose energy is absorbed can make electricity.

Solar Power in Space

Take a look at the International Space Station. What is it covered in? Solar panels! All the solar panels on the space station could cover one whole football field. This also makes the station the second-brightest object in the night sky. You can see pictures of the space station here.

space station solar panels NASA 🔎

Want to know when and where you can see the International Space Station? With a parent's permission, sign up for alerts from NASA.

spot the station 🔎

researcher: a person who systematically studies something.

carbon footprint: the total amount of carbon dioxide and other greenhouse gases emitted over the full life cycle of a product or service, or by a person, family, or community in a year.

concentrate: to bring or direct toward the center.

passive solar: use of the sun's energy to heat buildings or water.

WORDS TO KNOW

The biggest challenge in using solar energy is the efficiency of the panels. Scientists, **researchers**, and engineers are working to improve the design and efficiency of solar panels.

The solar panels from the 1950s were not very efficient. Back then, only 5 percent of the energy that reached a panel's surface was converted into electricity. That means 95 percent of the energy was being lost! Through research and innovation, engineers are constantly improving the efficiency of solar panel designs. A solar panel created in 2015 at the National Renewable Energy Laboratory in Colorado keeps up to 45 percent of the sun's energy.

The increased efficiency of solar panels means fewer panels are needed to power a house, business, or city. Consider the Solar Photovoltaic Power Plant in Tangtse, India. High in the Himalayas at nearly 14,500 feet, this power plant powers a remote village of about 400 homes. How efficient will solar panels be 50 years into the future?

PS

Solar Explorer

Bertrand Piccard, one of the men who flew on the *Solar Impulse*, was also the first person to fly a hot air balloon around the world. He says, "If what you are doing is easy, everyone else would have already done it." You can listen to an interview with him and see videos of the solar-powered plane.

Piccard airplane land rover 🔍

Solar energy is free. It produces no pollution and leaves no **carbon footprint**. This makes solar one of the renewables with the most potential to continue to grow.

Solar Thermal Energy

Engineers have designed another way to capture energy from the sun. Solar thermal energy turns the power of the sun into heat. There are two different types of solar thermal energy systems: **concentrated** solar power and **passive solar** power.

Researcher

Research jobs are key in the development of solar technology and other renewables. Researchers investigate problems using data. Solar researchers may study solar cells, photons, and materials used to make solar panels. Remember, we are still trying to create that super-efficient solar panel.

Concentrated solar power (CSP) uses mirrors to reflect a large area of sunlight onto a smaller area. The mirrors automatically track the sun throughout the day. Electricity is generated when the concentrated light heats up water and converts it to steam, powering a generator. CSP is mainly found in sunny states.

Ivanpah

There are different types of CSP plants. A solar power tower can produce temperatures of more than 900 degrees Fahrenheit. The largest solar power tower is the Ivanpah Solar Electric Generation System. Located in southern California, it uses three towers to produce enough electricity to power 100,000 homes.

turbine: a device that uses pressure on blades by water, air, or steam to spin generators and create electricity.

WORDS TO KNOW

The second type of CSP solar uses curved mirrors to reflect the sun's rays and convert water to steam. The mirrors are shaped like half-pipes and are 94 percent reflective.

The sunlight bounces off the mirrors and is directed to a central tube, which heats to more than 750 degrees Fahrenheit. The reflected light focused at the central tube is 80 times more intense than ordinary sunlight.

The heat in the tube is used to boil water. Then the steam turns a **turbine**, generating electricity. The Kramer Solar Power Junction facility in California, which uses this technology, can power up to 500,000 homes.

Plugged In

The U.S. Department of Energy in Washington, DC, has solar panels on its rooftop. More than 900 solar panels cover nearly 2,000 square feet on the roof to help power the building.

How do we capture the sun's energy with no electronics or wiring? It's called passive solar heat. This approach uses black surfaces or pipes to quickly heat water, called passive solar water heating. It is used in many places around the world. People run water through black pipes placed on the roofs of their homes to save energy.

Make a list of all the things you have to do when you use hot water for cooking or bathing. How does having the water warmed in pipes on your roof help save energy? Have you ever thought about where your hot water comes from?

Green Schools

There are more than 3,700 schools around the United States using solar technology! One of those is an elementary school in rural Bowling Green, Kentucky. The school is using solar panels to power its classrooms, gyms, and cafeteria. This won it an award: the first net-zero school in the United States. What is net zero? It means they produce all the energy they use. If they had an electric bill, it would be zero dollars!

Powering Our Lives With the Sun

Solar technologies are used around the world. From the first solar-paneled home built in the United States in 1948 in Massachusetts to the first solar panels on the White House installed under President Jimmy Carter in 1979, the solar industry has grown tremendously.

Businesses, homes, energy utilities, and schools are joining the solar revolution. More than 2.5 million students in the United States attend schools that use forms of solar technology.

GREEN JOBS

Green Business People

Are you interested in helping the solar industry grow? You might become a real estate agent, bank financier, or marketer for solar companies. All of these jobs have roles to play in helping people use solar. Real estate agents can help people learn about the value of a house with solar panels. Bankers help schools, businesses, and families get loans to install and maintain solar energy systems. Marketers are needed to help solar companies sell their products.

Solar power isn't just an environmental convenience. It can also can help save lives. In Africa and Asia, there are still millions of people living without electricity. The houses don't have light switches and power outlets. Many families still burn wood to heat their homes, cook their food, and light their homes at night.

Solar panels can change access to electricity.

Africa has an abundance of sunshine. Solar panels are a potential solution. However, there are two obstacles to making this the future of energy. We need engineers and scientists to design and manufacture the solar technology, and leaders who demand change.

With the abundance of sunshine on our planet, why aren't we creating more solar electricity? Solar is one of the fastest growing renewable energy technologies, but it still has a long way to go. Let's explore another renewable energy that has the potential to change the way we treat our planet—wind!

ESSENTIAL QUESTION

Now it's time to consider and discuss the Essential Question:
How can we use the sun to produce energy here on the earth?

Solar Energy Trade-offs

Solar energy offers incredible potential for the future. But no single energy source is perfect. Solar energy has pros, but also potential cons. What are the trade-offs of switching to solar energy?

First, solar energy can be unpredictable. While we have the ability to forecast weather, one can never be entirely certain what tomorrow's weather will be. If it is excessively cloudy or foggy, that reduces the amount of energy that solar panels produce. On cloudy days, solar panels generate power, just less of it. But what if it's cloudy for an entire week? It is possible that solar technology will not produce enough energy when we need it. We need ways to store solar energy for whenever the sun doesn't shine, such as cloudy days and nighttime.

We humans have come to rely on the predictability of our energy supply. What would happen if you couldn't run your computer or power your car? Can you think of who might be most affected by an unpredictable energy supply? Factories might be in the middle of making something, emergency workers could be using power to help someone, and elevators might be transporting people in tall buildings. We can all be impacted by fluctuations in energy supply.

Where we find solar energy is also an important consideration. Can you guess which areas have the most predictable weather for solar energy? If you guessed desert regions, you are correct. In the desert, there is less rain and less cloud cover. That makes America's Desert Southwest an incredible area for producing solar power.

Solar technology requires a large area to produce enough energy to power cities and towns. Solar fields that stretch over large areas can impact wildlife and scenery. When considering solar energy, city planners and utility companies have to consider how much space will be required.

One more consideration is the amount of metals required to build photovoltaic cells. Mining for metals impacts the land. And what happens to solar panels that are old and need to be scrapped? Can the materials be recycled?

What do you think? Is solar power worth the trade-off?

POWER OF SUNLIGHT

IDEAS FOR SUPPLIES

2 sheets of NaturePrint paper, available in art stores or online • dark-colored construction paper • toys, objects, cut-out paper shapes • plastic bag • sunscreen

We know sunlight helps plants grow, evaporates water, causes sunburn, provides energy, and gives us light to see. We know that sunlight can help power our activities, from outer space to inside our own homes. But how powerful is the sunlight? This activity uses sun-sensitive paper to help you explore the power of the sun. You need a sunny day to do this activity!

1 Place a piece of dark construction paper and a piece of NaturePrint paper directly in the sun. Keep pieces of the same paper inside.

2 Place your toys, objects, and cut-out paper shapes on the construction paper and NaturePrint paper. Try creating a pattern on the paper.

3 What do you think will happen to the paper? To the objects? Think about the heat and the light coming from the sun. Write your predictions in your science journal.

4 After about 45 minutes, compare the construction paper, the NaturePrint paper, and the papers inside. How are they different?

Plugged In

Cities absorb a lot of solar energy because of all the black surfaces on roads and buildings, so they often are hotter than the surrounding countryside. This is why scientists call cities "heat islands."

WORDS TO KNOW

evaporate: when a liquid heats up and changes into a gas.

5 Dip the NaturePrint paper in water and then let it dry. What happens? How are the papers different? How are they similar? What caused the differences? What might happen on a cloudy day?

TRY THIS: How does sunscreen protect us? Put half of the NaturePrint paper in a plastic bag. Leave half exposed to the sun. Use sunscreen to cover the half of the paper exposed to the sun for 45 minutes. Remove it from the sun and place it in water, then wait for it to dry. What happened to the paper that was in the plastic bag? What happened to the parts covered in sunscreen? Record your observations in your science journal.

SOLAR THERMAL ENERGY

IDEAS FOR SUPPLIES
Post-it Notes • *3 thermometers* • *white and black paper*

How are heat and light related? Begin by creating a table that will help you organize data. In this activity, you will write down the temperatures, your prediction, and results from different thermometers.

1 Label your thermometers 1, 2, and 3 using the Post-it Notes.

2 Which thermometer do you think will get the hottest—the one on black paper, the one under white paper, or the one that's just lying in the sun? Write down your prediction in your science journal. Create a chart to record your **observations**.

Thermometer	Prediction	Actual Temperature

3 Place the three thermometers in the sun. Place the bulb of thermometer 1 on a piece of black paper. Place a piece of white paper over the bulb of thermometer 2. Leave thermometer 3 uncovered in the sun.

4 After 3 minutes, record the temperatures in your science journal. What color paper absorbed more of the sun's energy?

THINK ABOUT IT:

How does the color of your clothing impact how hot you get? Should you wear darker or lighter clothing if it is hot? How might the color of the seats in your car impact the heat in your car?

WORDS TO KNOW

prediction: what you think will happen.

observation: something you notice.

Chapter 2

FARMING THE WIND

> **Did you know that the sun is responsible for the wind? Wind energy is really just another type of solar energy. Wind is air in motion, produced by the uneven heating of the earth's surface by the sun. As the sun warms the earth's surface, the atmosphere also warms.**

Wind energy relies on great height. Wind engineers are building taller and taller wind turbines because the higher the wind turbine reaches off the ground, the more energy it produces. The challenge of building bigger wind turbines requires the collaboration of scientists and engineers from around the world.

? ESSENTIAL QUESTION

Why do we think of wind as another form of solar energy?

As you watch the exciting development in the construction of wind turbines, keep in mind that wind is found in all 50 states of the United States. Wind is found in every country around the globe.

What Is Wind?

As you can imagine, some parts of the earth are warmer than others. If you live near the **equator**, you receive more direct sun rays than any other place on earth. Farther north and south of the equator, the sun warms the surface less. That is why it is hotter at the equator than at the North Pole.

As air warms, it expands.

This means warm air is less **dense** than cold air. Because warm air is less dense, it rises. This is how hot air balloons work! As the balloon fills with hot air, the area inside the balloon becomes less dense and rises above the heavier, colder air around it.

When the warm air rises, it leaves an area of low pressure. Cooler air moves in underneath to balance the pressure.

Plugged In

Traditional power plants use a lot of water, but power plants using wind don't need water. This means that wind energy helps to **conserve** water resources. Mathematicians predict that by the year 2050, wind energy can save 260 billion gallons of water. That amount of water could fill 400,000 Olympic-size swimming pools.

This movement of warm air and cool air is what makes the wind blow. Predictable differences in temperature at the surface of the earth cause predictable global wind patterns.

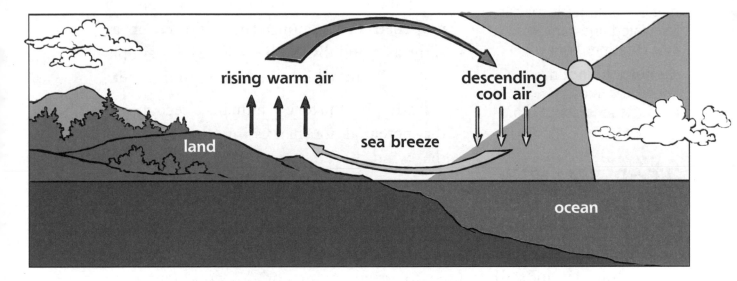

Where Can We Find Wind?

You might notice that different areas of your town or city absorb more solar energy than others. Light-colored surfaces and water reflect more sunlight than dark surfaces, so those areas are cooler. Snow and ice reflect sunlight, too. Some types of land absorb more solar energy than others. Buildings and roads usually absorb more energy than lakes and oceans. The sun's heat can cause wind patterns even at the local level.

Some places have more wind than others. The air over deserts gets warmer than the air in the mountains. The air over the land usually gets warmer than the air over the water. When warm air rises and cool air takes its place, those areas get wind. As long as the sun shines, there will be wind on the earth.

Windmill to Wind Turbine

People have harnessed the energy of the wind for thousands of years. Wind energy propelled boats along the Nile River as early as 5000 BCE. By 200 BCE, simple windmills in China were pumping water.

Early in history, humans recognized the potential for harvesting the power of the wind to do meaningful work. Early American farmers and colonists used windmills to grind wheat and corn, pump water, and cut wood at sawmills. Today, we use the wind to generate electricity. A wind turbine is used to make electricity, while a windmill is used to grind, pump, or do work, but does not generate electricity.

A wind turbine consists of four main parts—the tower, blades, shaft, and generator. When the wind blows, it pushes against the blades of the wind turbines, causing them to spin around. As the blades spin, they cause a giant magnet in the turbine to spin. We measure wind speeds using anemometers.

PS

Windy Schools

Towns County Schools in Hiawassee, Georgia, are using a wind turbine to power their school campus. The school campus has an elementary, middle, and high school, all powered by wind! Use this interactive map to find out where other wind energy projects are happening in the United States. From K–12 schools to museums and community colleges, wind projects are being used all over the country.

windexchange school projects 🔍

Manufacturing

Factories that once created the steel, nails, and bolts for our railroads are now creating wind turbine parts. From the rotor blades to the towers and gearboxes, there are many parts needed to make a wind turbine work. There are more than 500 wind-related **manufacturing** facilities across 43 states in the country. Building wind turbine parts is an important job if we are going to use wind to power our lives. GE Energy is the largest wind turbine manufacturer in the United States.

The spinning magnet surrounded by copper wire is what generates electricity. The tower is what holds the blades and enables us to access that wind high up in the sky. A brand new wind turbine can have as many as 8,000 parts.

The size of wind turbines has steadily grown larger. The average height of land-based turbines increased 46 percent from 1998 to 2013. Why do you think that is?

During World War II, the largest wind turbine was 110 feet tall with 75-foot blades. It could generate enough electricity to light 1,600 homes. Today's largest wind turbine is 720 feet tall with 260-foot blades. It can power up to 7,500 homes. This wind turbine can create up to 800 percent more electricity!

Inside a wind turbine, mechanical elements cause magnets to spin, generating electricity.

The largest turbine's blades cover an area equal to four of the world's largest passenger planes.

Designing Wind Turbines

Wind turbines used to generate electricity have changed a lot through time. One of the biggest changes has been the size and design of the rotor blades. Longer blades produce more electricity, but as the blades get longer, the tower must get higher. This is called a direct relationship. As one increases, the other increases, too. As blades get bigger and towers get taller, the cost to generate electricity falls. This is called an inverse relationship.

There are many different designs for wind turbines, but all of them fall into one of two categories—horizontal or vertical axis of rotation. A horizontal axis wind turbine is the more traditional design that looks like a large propeller.

GREEN JOBS

Project Manager

Project managers work hand in hand with wind energy engineers to help identify wind site locations and manage wind energy business opportunities. Environmental regulations, permits, and research are often conducted by wind project managers. This occurs before wind energy can be deployed in new areas. Engineers help design and prepare the new sites for wind farms.

A vertical axis wind turbine is more useful in urban and low-lying areas where the direction of the wind is frequently changing. The blades spin around like a carousel at the amusement park.

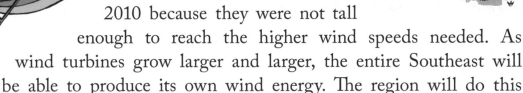

Vertical Turbine

As engineers design taller towers, more areas are able to access wind energy. Wind turbines in the southeastern United States were not economical in 2010 because they were not tall enough to reach the higher wind speeds needed. As wind turbines grow larger and larger, the entire Southeast will be able to produce its own wind energy. The region will do this by capturing wind at higher altitudes, using the larger wind turbines than are now available.

Today, wind-powered generators operate in every size range, from small turbines for individual homes to large wind farms that provide electricity for entire cities, and even countries. Those monster wind turbines are great for powering cities, but you can also use small wind turbines to power individual homes. Both large and small wind turbines are cost-effective and give off no pollution.

Horizontal Turbine

Green Schools

Kirkwood Community College in Iowa has a three-blade wind turbine. Each blade weighs up to 30,000 pounds. The power from the turbine is sold to utility company, which provides about $300,000 a year for the college. The wind turbine is being used as a living-learning laboratory for students in the energy production and distribution technologies program.

archaeologist: a scientist who studies ancient people through the objects they left behind.

wind farm: groups or clusters of wind turbines that produce large amounts of electricity together.

smart grid: a computer-based remote control and automated system for electricity delivery. It includes two-way interaction between the generation facilities, utilities, and consumers.

WORDS TO KNOW

Farming the Wind

Humans have been farming for more than 12,000 years. Archaeological records suggest that the first example of farming was in the Tigris and Euphrates River Delta. This is in modern-day Iraq. **Archaeologists** have found examples of farming on every continent and in all types of environments. Farming is important for food and jobs around the world.

On April 17, 1980, a new type of farming was invented—wind farming! A **wind farm** or wind park is a group of wind turbines installed in the same location, used to produce electricity. There are two types of wind farms. Onshore wind farms are the type where the wind turbine is placed solidly on dry ground. Offshore wind turbines are anchored directly to the ocean floor or float above the ocean floor.

A large wind farm might consist of several hundred individual wind turbines and cover hundreds of square miles. The land between the turbines can still be used for agricultural or other purposes.

Plugged In

It would take nearly 4,000 five-megawatt turbines to help power New York City. The wind turbines would take up about 40-by-40 square miles. This was calculated by Professor Paul Sclavounos, a professor of mechanical engineering and naval architecture.

Wind farmers plant giant wind turbines just as agriculture farmers plant rows of corn.

Wind farms generate so much electricity that they can power entire cities. They can connect directly to the smart grid. Since that first wind farm was created in 1980, more than 1,000 wind farm projects have been built in the world, with more than 48,000 individual wind turbines in the United States.

Eight of the 10 largest wind farms in the world are operated in America. Texas has five large wind farms. The Alta Wind Energy Center in California is the largest wind farm in the United States, with the capacity to produce 1,320 megawatts of power. That is enough electricity to power a million homes. The Department of Energy estimates that wind power in the United States could provide enough electricity to meet 30 percent of all the country's electricity needs by 2050.

PS Mapping Wind Farms

You can investigate wind farm growth both globally and in the United States by using these two interactive maps.

Use the scroll bar to compare past years to today. What do you notice about the rate of change?

global wind energy council map 🔍 — AWEA maps 🔍

Currently, wind farms produce enough energy to power more than 15 million homes in America. That is the electricity equivalent to burning 320 million barrels of oil every year.

Wind power delivers public health and environmental benefits today. These include reduced greenhouse gas emissions, reduced air pollutants, and reduced water consumption. Wind technology provides a domestic, sustainable, and essentially pollution-free electricity resource.

Plugged In

Micro-windmills are the size of a grain of rice. They can be used to power small objects such as smartphones and clocks. Micro-windmills are being built at the University of Texas at Arlington.

Environmental Benefits from Wind Generation in 2013

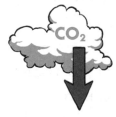

Carbon dioxide reduced by
115,000,000
metric tons

Equivalent to
CO_2 emissions from
270 million
barrels of oil

Sulfur dioxide reduced by
157,000
metric tons

Equivalent to annual emissions of
12 coal plants

Nitrogen oxide reduced by
97,000
metric tons

Equivalent to annual emissions of
10 coal plants

Water consumption reduced by
36.5 billion
gallons

Equivalent to
116 gallons/ person
in the United States

What happens when the wind doesn't blow? This is one of the reasons people shouldn't rely on a single renewable energy source. We need to use a variety of sources that complement each other. Let's check out how water power uses turbines in our next chapter.

? ESSENTIAL QUESTION

Now it's time to consider and discuss the Essential Question: Why do we think of wind as another form of solar energy?

ENERGY TRADE-OFFS

Wind Energy Trade-offs

Wind power, like solar power, can be unpredictable. This is one reason towns and cities don't run on just solar power or just wind power. Our lives require a predictable energy supply.

One of the major trade-offs for wind energy is the impact wind turbines have on migrating birds. Because wind turbines can spin at more than 200 miles per hour at the tips of the blades, faster than many race cars, birds that are flying near them are in danger of being struck. There are not exact numbers on how many birds are injured or killed every year by wind turbines, but there is a logical concern about their impact.

Another issue with wind turbines is that some people feel they negatively impact the scenic beauty of the landscape. Of course beauty is in the eye of the beholder: One person may see a wind turbine as an eyesore, while another person may see a turbine as a beautiful sign of progress and clean energy.

A final consideration is that wind turbines have been known to create a whooshing noise when spinning. People who live near wind turbines can be impacted by the constant sound. Would you want to live near a turbine if it was always making a whooshing sound?

Despite these issues, wind technology provides a domestic, sustainable, and essentially pollution-free electricity resource. Can you live with the trade-offs?

WIND CAN DO WORK

IDEAS FOR SUPPLIES

large foam cup • extra-wide straw • narrow straw • masking tape • 4-blade windmill template • 2 straight pins • string or thread • paper clips • binder clip • fan • hole punch • marker

Use your engineering skills to design a windmill, then test how powerful the wind can be.

1 Turn the cup upside down. Cut the wide straw to 3 inches in length. Use a ruler to measure the length.

2 Tape the straw horizontally on the top of the cup so there is an equal amount of straw on both sides.

3 Use the windmill blade templates to make your windmill blades. You can find the templates at **nomadpress.net/templates**.

4 Measure a half inch from the end of the narrow straw and make a mark.

5 Insert a pin through the narrow straw at this mark. This is the front of the straw.

6 Slide the narrow straw through the windmill blades until the back of the blades rest against the pin. Gently slide each blade over the end of the straw. Secure the blades to the straw using tape.

7 Insert the narrow straw into the wider straw on the cup. Tape the string to the end of the small straw. Tie the other end of the string to a paper clip. Make sure you have 12 inches of string from the straw to the top of the paper clip.

8 On the very end of the narrow straw, near where the string is attached, fasten a binder clip in place for balance and to keep the string winding around the straw.

9 Slide the narrow straw forward to bring the binder clip next to the wider straw. Place a second straight pin through the narrow straw at the other end of the wider straw. This will keep the blades away from the cup while still allowing them to move and spin.

10 Place your windmill in front of the fan. How does it work? Is there anything you can do to improve the design? Record your observations in your science journal.

TRY THIS: If you had to redesign your blades, what would you do differently? Why? Redesign your blades. What shapes work best? What else can you use to attach the parts to each other? Test your new designs. Note your observations and compare the designs in your science journal.

GLIDER CONTEST

IDEAS FOR SUPPLIES

paper • templates

In this activity, you will design paper airplane gliders to experiment with the effects of wind. Do this experiment on a windy day with friends.

1 Make three different glider patterns using the templates for Master Glider, High Glider, and Flying Wing. For templates and more detailed instructions go to **nomadpress.net/templates**.

2 To create the Master Glider, take a piece of 8½-by-11-inch paper. Cut off the bottom 2 inches using a ruler to measure. Fold the paper in half lengthwise and fold the top down 1½ inches.

3 Fold the top two corners down to the center, creating an airplane look. Fold the wings down and tape them together. Bend the wings up a little to help with the glide.

4 To make the High Glider, fold another piece of 8½-by-11-inch paper in half lengthwise. Open it back up but make sure you can see the crease.

5 Fold the top two corners down into the center. Fold the point down to the crease you created. Fold the top two corners to the center and fold it lengthwise in half. It should look like a plane. Fold out the wings in your own design and you have your High Glider ready to test.

6 To make the Flying Wing, fold a piece of 8½-by-11-inch paper in half lengthwise. Fold the top third of the paper down from the open end. Fold the top down again to the bottom of the previous fold. Now fold the paper in half away from you. Fold down the wings and design them so they look like they can fly.

7 Now that your gliders are all built, examine them. Which glider do you think will fly the farthest? Write your hypothesis in your science journal.

8 Test each glider design you make. Try to throw the gliders all the same way so you can compare them. Which one flies the farthest? Why?

THINK ABOUT IT: The lifting force that lifts the gliders is the same force that acts on the blades of wind turbines and makes them spin. What can you learn about the shape of wind turbines by testing different shapes of gliders?

ELECTRIC MOTOR

IDEAS FOR SUPPLIES

small neodymium disk magnet (from a small plastic toy, for example)
• drywall screw • 6 inches plain copper wire • 1.5-volt battery

This activity will help you see how electricity is generated. Electricity is sometimes called an energy carrier. It moves energy from one place to another.

1 Place the top of the screw on the magnet, vertically. The magnet should hold onto the screw. Bend the wire into the shape of a capital letter L.

2 Hold the battery with the button side down. Touch the tip of the screw opposite the end with the magnet to the button end of the battery. The battery, screw, and magnet should all hold onto each other.

3 Take the wire and press it on the opposite end of the battery. This makes an electrical connection between the top of the battery and the wire.

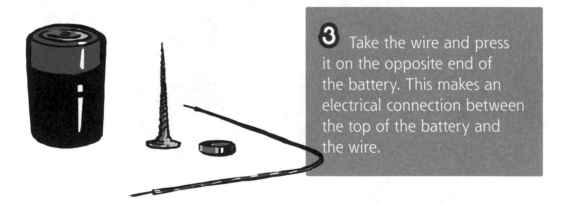

4 Using the free end of the wire touch the side of the magnet gently. What happens? Now pull the wire away and observe what happens. Try this several times.

ACTIVITY

44

5 You have just completed an electric circuit. The energy flows from the battery, down the screw, sideways through the magnet to the wire and to the other end of the battery.

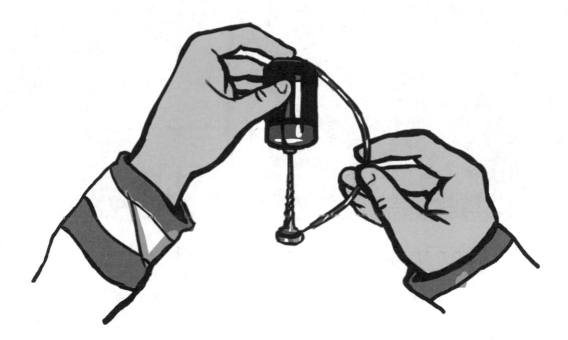

THINK ABOUT IT: You just built a basic electric motor. How long do you think electric motors have been used in the car industry? Write your answer in your journal. You might be surprised with what you find out if you search online for "History of Electric Car." Write down what you discover in your journal.

Chapter 3

PLANET WATER

**From space, our planet looks like a blue marble.
That is because nearly 70 percent of the
surface of the earth is covered in water.**

As far as we know, Earth is the only planet in our solar system whose surface always has liquid water on it. That makes our world a pretty special place, since liquid water is what supports life. Solid water is known to exist on the moon, deep in craters and underground. Scientists exploring Mars have discovered evidence of flowing water just under the surface.

? ESSENTIAL QUESTION

What methods can we use to harness the power of moving water?

Venus might once have had water, but because of something called the **runaway greenhouse effect**, the surface of Venus is now more than 700 degrees Fahrenheit. At this temperature, any water that existed on Venus would have boiled away into the atmosphere.

Plugged In

There is enough water in the oceans to fill about 352,670 trillion gallon-size milk containers! At any given moment, the atmosphere contains approximately 37.5 million billion gallons of water, or 37.5 quadrillion gallons.

If Venus ever cools down, much of the water trapped in its atmosphere could fall back as rain.

We use water every day, to bathe in, to cook in, and to drink. The ocean provides food, medicines, minerals, and energy resources. Water supports jobs, tourism, farming, and, of course, swimming! Water can also be used to move goods from one place to another and generate electricity. In this chapter, we'll explore some of the inventions helping us convert the energy from water into energy we can use to do other things.

Look Up!

Why is the sky blue? When we look up on a sunny day, we see a blue sky because light from the sun travels through oxygen and nitrogen molecules in the atmosphere to get to the earth. Light energy travels in waves of different colors and wavelengths. Those waves are scattered when they pass through the molecules. Blue waves are scattered more than other colors because their wavelengths are shorter. That's why we see blue!

evaporation: when the surface of a liquid changes from a liquid to a gas.

water vapor: the gaseous form of water in the air.

hydrokinetic: the motion of fluids.

hydropower: energy produced by the movement of water.

byproduct: an extra and sometimes unexpected or unintended result of an action or process.

hydroelectric power plant: a power plant that uses moving water to power a turbine generator to produce electricity.

WORDS TO KNOW

The Power of H₂O

Water is constantly moving. Think about all the water sources you know—oceans, lakes, rivers, the creek behind your back yard, and even that frozen glacier you might have seen on television. They all move. The water in some have currents, such as in rivers and streams. The water in others move through **evaporation**, such as in lakes and ponds.

Plugged In

When it's a hot, humid day during the summer, you sweat a lot. Humidity is the measurement of **water vapor** in the air.

It's easy to picture rivers moving, but what about glaciers? How do they move? Glaciers are actually slow-moving rivers of ice. You usually can't see them move just by watching them, but if you measure their progress during a long period of time, you can tell that they are moving.

The energy of moving water is called **hydrokinetic** energy. It is the most widely used form of renewable energy in the world. Hydrokinetic energy accounts for almost 50 percent of all renewable energy generation. The power that results from hydrokinetic energy is called **hydropower**. Hydropower is produced in 150 countries and is one of the oldest power sources on the planet.

**Hydropower produces
no air pollution or toxic byproducts.**

Every state in the United States uses hydropower for electricity. Some states use a lot of it. In Washington, 70 percent of the electricity comes from hydropower. Eleven states get more than 10 percent of their electricity from hydropower. China is the largest hydroelectricity producer in the world.

Modern Hydropower

The evolution of modern hydropower began in the mid-1700s with the invention of the turbine. You learned in the last chapter that the turbine is very important for generating electricity from wind. It is also needed for creating electricity from the movement of water.

The first water turbine was created in 1880. It was used to make an electric spark to provide light for a theater and storefront in Grand Rapids, Michigan. In 1881, a water turbine in a flour mill provided street lighting in Niagara Falls, New York.

Hydropower has seen a number of advancements in the past century. This includes the creation of hydroelectric power plants.

PS

Map It

There are about 75,000 dams in the national database of the U.S. Army Corp of Engineers. You can see where they are on an online interactive map. What parts of the country have the most dams? What parts have the least? Why?

national inventory dams interactive map 🔍

kinetic: the movement of physical objects.

flow: the amount of water that moves through a hydropower plant.

water cycle: the movement of water from land to bodies of water, into the atmosphere, and back to the earth.

condense: when a gas cools down and changes into a liquid.

gravitational effect: the force of attraction between two masses.

WORDS TO KNOW

The first U.S. hydroelectric power plant opened on the Fox River near Appleton, Wisconsin, on September 30, 1882. Since that time, we have relied mostly on dams in rivers to create hydropower.

Sea Snakes

Scientists and engineers are always designing new ways to generate electricity using water. Inventions such as underwater turbines can capture the currents in rivers and oceans. Engineers have developed buoy systems made from super magnets that rise and fall with the tides and waves and generate electricity. Tidal generators make use of the **kinetic** energy of moving water to power turbines. Similar to wind turbines, tidal turbines use the **flow** of water caused by rising and falling tides to make their turbines spin. We also can capture energy from waves, using uniquely designed devices such as sea snakes that float on top of the water.

Underwater Wind Turbines

We have explored less than 5 percent of the oceans. There is still a lot to learn about the water that covers most of our planet. The oceans could help to cleanly power us into the next century and beyond.

The Force Behind the Tides

Have you ever walked on the beach and seen the beach get smaller or larger during the course of a day? Every 12 hours and 52 minutes, there is a rotation from high tide to low tide on the earth. Tides play a major role in our ability to use energy from the water.

Tidal power, or tidal energy, is another form of hydropower. Tides are the periodic rising and falling of large bodies of water. Tidal power can be converted into electricity. There is incredible potential in tidal power because tides are more predictable than wind energy and solar power.

Plugged In

The **water cycle** is the endless process that water travels through on Earth. It evaporates to become water vapor in clouds. Then it **condenses** into liquid water in the form of rain or snow, over and over again. The amount of water in the water cycle has remained constant for the last 300 million years. That means the water you drink today is the same water the dinosaurs drank.

The moon, sun, and the earth's rotation are responsible for the tides. However, the moon is closest and has the most effect. It is an eighth of the mass of the earth and 250,000 miles away. Even at that distance, the moon has a large **gravitational effect** on the earth.

As the moon revolves around the earth every 27 days, 7 hours, 43 minutes, and 11.6 seconds, the earth's gravity causes water to bulge on the near and far sides of the planet.

dam: a wall built across a waterway to stop water flow.

reservoir: a natural or manmade body of water stored for future use.

WORDS TO KNOW

On the side of the planet facing the moon, water bulges because the moon's gravity is pulling on it. On the side of the planet not facing the moon, water bulges because as the moon's gravity pulls on the earth,

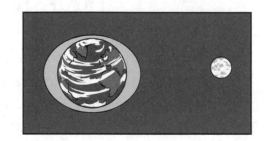

the water on the far side is left with less pull and bulges out. This happens every day of the year. What would happen to the tides on the planet if the moon suddenly disappeared?

Sun and Water

We know that the moon causes the tides. The sun also affects the tides, but to a much lesser extent since it's so far away. What other effect does the sun have on water? The sun is responsible for the water cycle. This cycle is what causes rain and snow. Rain and snowfall replenish our rivers, lakes, and mountain snowpack. Without the water cycle, these would all run dry.

Hydrologists and Hydropower Engineers

Hydrologists help study the movement of water. They analyze soil, look at the physical properties of ground and surface waters, and study precipitation. Their work helps us understand the power of water. Hydropower engineers help create hydroelectric projects. The engineers work with environmental scientists to address environmental issues. Hydroelectric projects include building major **dams**, creating **reservoirs**, and constructing power plants.

**Without the water cycle,
all water would end up in the oceans
and never return to land.**

Water always flows downhill because of gravity. How does the water get back up to the top of the hill? How do streams stay full if water is constantly flowing down? Water in the ocean evaporates and becomes water vapor in the atmosphere. Eventually, this water vapor falls back to the earth in the form of rain or snow. It flows back to the rivers and eventually to the ocean. A drop of water in the ocean can take anywhere from a day to 3,000 years to evaporate and fall back to the earth as rain.

Without the water cycle, we would live in a world without lakes, ponds, rivers, glaciers, and snow, and we wouldn't have any need for dams. What else would be missing from a world without the water cycle?

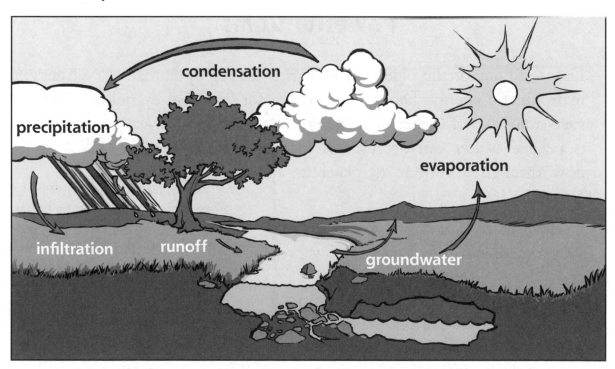

topsoil: the top layer of soil.

irrigation: to provide water for crops through ditches, pipes, and other means.

pump storage: a system for moving water using extra electricity, storing the water, then allowing the water to flow through turbines to create electricity when it's needed.

WORDS TO KNOW

How do we know how much water there is on the earth? One way is by measuring the amount of water in the top 2 inches of soil everywhere on the earth's surface. NASA's Soil Moisture Active Passive (SMAP) is a satellite in space that collects data on the amount of moisture in **topsoil**. The topsoil layer is where we grow food and where plants live.

SMAP is designed to measure soil moisture every two or three days during a three-year period. It gathers data every time the satellite loops around the world. This provides scientists with repeated measurements of changes in soil moisture month after month, season after season, year after year. The data helps us understand the movement of water on earth.

Powerful Dams

Dams are one of the oldest technologies created by humans to harness hydrokinetic energy. Dams store energy for later use by holding back vast amounts of water. As energy is needed, water can be released to flow through a turbine to generate electricity.

Most dams are found on rivers. When people think of hydropower and dams, they might imagine structures such as the Hoover Dam on the Arizona-Nevada border or the Glen Canyon Dam in Arizona. Wisconsin was the site of the country's first hydroelectric generating facility, built in 1882.

Plugged In

The Three Gorges Dam in Hubei Province, China, is the world's largest dam. It was completed in 2009 and is located on the Yangtze River. Three Gorges Dam holds back more than 5 trillion gallons of water.

The Hoover Dam and Glen Canyon Dam are massive structures. These engineering marvels store the power of the mighty Colorado River behind their walls.

Hydropower facilities can also be tiny and placed anywhere water flows. In the United States, we produce clean, renewable electricity from roughly 2,500 dams. The country also has more than 80,000 non-powered dams, or dams that do not produce electricity at all.

Why would engineers build a dam if it does not produce electricity? What other uses can dams provide? Dams can be used to help store water for irrigation, to create new lakes for recreational purposes, and to control flooding on rivers. Using new, modern technology, many of these 80,000 dams can be converted into energy-producing facilities.

Pump Storage

What do engineers do when they generate lots of extra electricity? They save it with pump storage. It used to be that if you didn't use the electricity you produced from renewable energy sources, you'd lose it. What a waste! In an effort to save this precious energy, engineers use something called pump storage.

When a power plant produces more energy than is being consumed, engineers use the extra energy to pump water uphill into a reservoir. Here, the water waits. Later, when the energy is needed, the water is allowed to flow back downhill through a turbine, producing electricity.

Pump storage of water is a critical part of our renewable energy future. There will be days with lots of sunshine when solar panels create excess energy. There will also be days with lots of wind when wind farms produce more energy than can be immediately used.

This pumping technology makes sure that the extra energy we harness on very sunny or windy days can be stored and used when needed.

All of these hydropower inventions show us how powerful water really is. Life on earth is linked to water and our existence is dependent on water. You could say that our whole civilization is built on the use of water. This makes water a great renewable energy competitor in the energy Olympics.

Humans have been harnessing water to perform work for thousands of years. The future for designing new innovative ways of harnessing electricity from water is limited only by our imaginations. This helps us move farther away from our reliance on fossil fuels. Fossil fuel extraction has a long history of polluting our water resources. But we now live in a world where we know how to harness the energy of the oceans, tides, rivers, wind, and the sun.

We even know how to harness energy that comes from the center of the earth. We'll explore geothermal energy in the next chapter.

ESSENTIAL QUESTION

Now it's time to consider and discuss the Essential Question: What methods can we use to harness the power of moving water?

ENERGY TRADE-OFFS

Water Energy Trade-offs

Power from the movement of water is the most abundantly utilized source of renewable energy in the world. But what kinds of impacts does using water to generate electricity have?

The use of dams is common around the world. Dams are used for irrigation, making electricity, gathering water, controlling flooding, and recreation. Dams stop the natural flow of rivers. The spawning grounds of certain species of fish have been known to be completely cut off because of dams on rivers. Damming a river also changes the amount of nutrients that flows downstream. This can impact living things for up to a thousand miles, sometimes even affecting the ocean ecosystem where rivers discharge.

Similar to solar energy, the area affected by the creation of a dam is often extremely large. The larger the dam, the larger the area that is flooded behind the dam. The flooding can impact our communities. When the Three Gorges Dam in China was created, millions of people had to move from their ancestral homes. The dam flooded more than 10 cities, 100 towns, and 1,000 villages in China.

Countries are using new guidelines to help weigh the pros and cons of dam projects. The type of dam and materials used impact the environment. Engineers think about the location, temperature, weather conditions, and depth of water when building a dam. Guidelines from the World Commission on Dams provides a framework for governments to evaluate the social, environmental, political, and financial impacts of dam projects. This analysis helps countries determine if the benefits outweigh the environmental impacts.

Systems that capture the energy in the tides and currents of the oceans have impacts on aquatic ecosystems. From the material used to make them to impacts on the ocean floor, there are some challenges in capturing the ocean's energy. Salt water causes corrosion in metal parts. Sea snakes might be hard to see by boats. Installing a sea snake or water turbine disrupts the ocean floor. More research and new designs using different materials will help us capture the ocean's energy. Engineers are designing new technologies to solve many of the issues with hydroelectric tools.

FORCE OF WATER

IDEAS FOR SUPPLIES
2-liter soda bottle • ruler • permanent marker • pushpin
• duct tape • paint tray • towel or paper towels

Imagine you are dam engineer, asked to build a new hydroelectric dam for your city. How high should your dam be? Does the height of the dam really make a difference? How does the volume of water behind the dam affect its power output?

1 Mark the bottle with a dot and horizontal line at 5, 10, 15, and 20 centimeters. Measure from the bottom of the soda bottle.

2 Use the pushpin to make a hole at the 5 centimeter mark only. Put a piece of duct tape over the hole. Fill the bottle with water to the 20 centimeter mark.

3 Place the bottle at one end of the paint tray with the hole pointing into the pan. Place the ruler at the base of the bottle and make marks on the bottom of the pan at 6-centimeter increments until you reach the end of the pan. In your science journal, make a table to record the distances for each trial.

4 Remove the duct tape and immediately measure the distance the water projects out from the hole. Record your measurement. Repeat this experiment two more times and record your results.

5 Do the experiment again, but fill the bottle up to 5, 10, and 15 centimeters. Repeat three times for each amount of water and record the data you collect. At what distance did the water have the most force? At what distance did it have the least? How much water was in the bottle at those distances?

THINK ABOUT IT:

What would the ideal conditions be to get the most energy out of the water when designing a dam? Use words and diagrams to explain your thinking. Draw a design for the most efficient dam you can think of.

Plugged In

The Bay of Fundy is found on the northeast end of the Gulf of Maine between the Canadian provinces of New Brunswick and Nova Scotia on the Atlantic Ocean. This place has the highest tidal range on the planet. Because of the bay's size and shape, the tides go up and down as much as 53 feet between high and low tide.

ACTIVITY

LAND AND WATER

IDEAS FOR SUPPLIES
sand or soil • aluminum disposable rectangle pan • ruler • cup or bucket

In this activity, we'll examine the impacts water can have on land. We will create our own miniature experiment to do this. To do this experiment, you will need to go outside.

1 Read through the instructions. What do you think is going to happen to the soil? Record your hypothesis in your science journal.

2 Poke a hole about the thickness of a pencil in the side of your disposable aluminum cooking pan. The hole should be just above the bottom of the pan.

3 Put some sand and soil into your pan. Make sure the mixture is about 2 inches deep in the pan. Smooth the top of the sand or soil with your hand or ruler.

4 Raise one end of the pan using a rock or piece of wood. It should be higher on one side than on the other.

5 Fill the cup with water. Slowly pour water onto the dirt along one spot on the top edge of your pan.

6 What happens to the soil? Why? In your science journal, explain your results. How can you use your observations to explain the water cycle?

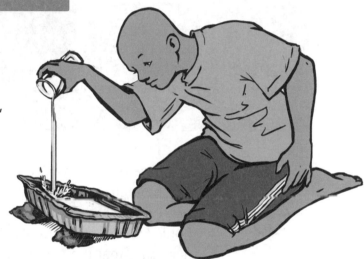

TRY THIS: Repeat this experiment and add rocks to your pan of soil. What happens? Does the soil move as much? Different types of land have to be considered when hydropower engineers build dams and reservoirs.

WATER CAN DO WORK

IDEAS FOR SUPPLIES

foam craft ball • sharpened pencil • glue • material for windmill blades • 2 disposable cups • 30 centimeters of thread • paper clips

In this activity, create your own watermill to see how the power of water can help create electricity. The blades on a watermill are what make it spin, and you will be designing your own blades.

1 Make a hole through the middle of the foam ball with a pencil. Slide the foam ball to the middle of the pencil. Place rings of glue on either side to secure the ball to the pencil.

2 You are going to insert four windmill blades into the foam ball at equal distances from each other. Think about what shape the blades should be and what you can make them out of. Make sure that the blades are not too long to fit into the cup.

3 Cut two small V-shaped grooves on opposite sides of the top of the cup.

4 Tie one end of a piece of thread to a paper clip. Tape the other end of the thread to the pencil.

5 Place the pencil into the grooves on the cup so the foam ball is in the center of the cup. Adjust and re-glue the blades so that they do not hit the edge of the cup.

Batteries and Energy

Engineers use batteries to store energy. The type of material used to create the battery impacts the storage and flow of that energy. In designing batteries, engineers examine characteristics such as size, safety, cost, ability to be recycled, and heat generation.

6 When the glue on the blades is dry, place the water wheel system at the edge of a table so the paper clip hangs off the table.

7 Get a second cup and fill it nearly full with water. Pour the water slowly and evenly onto the blades.

8 What happens after you pour water on the blades? Record your observations in your science journal.

Think About It:

How can you improve your water wheel design? What shape of blade might work better? Remake your water wheel and compare your results.

Chapter 4

MOTHER EARTH'S BEATING HEART

One of the hottest new renewable energy technologies is geothermal energy. Geothermal energy is heat from deep inside the earth. It is a clean, renewable resource that provides energy around the world.

There is evidence of the earth's inner heat everywhere. Have you ever seen volcanoes or hot springs? These are examples of the power of the energy beneath the ground.

? ESSENTIAL QUESTION

What is geothermal energy and how can we make it useful?

The heat of the earth is available everywhere. If we drill deep into the earth's crust, we can find enough thermal energy to power entire cities and towns. Engineers and scientists are working to design ways to use this energy to improve our efficiency and generate clean electricity.

As our geothermal technology improves, it has the potential to change the world for the better. To more clearly understand how and where to explore for geothermal energy, we will need to dig deeper into our knowledge of the earth.

hot spring: a natural pool of water that is heated by hot or molten rock. Hot springs are found in areas with active volcanoes.

mineral: a naturally occurring solid found in rocks and in the ground. Rocks are made of minerals. Gold and diamonds are precious minerals.

geyser: a hot spring under pressure that shoots boiling water or steam into the air.

WORDS TO KNOW

Plugged In

In North America, archaeological evidence shows that the first human use of geothermal resources occurred more than 10,000 years ago. Native American tribes established their homes near volcanic hot springs. The springs served as sources of warmth and their **minerals** were sources of healing.

Geothermal is a renewable resource because heat from inside the earth is limitless.

It's Hot Inside!

For thousands of years, people have known about the beauty and power of geothermal energy. Ancient Greeks even believed in a pair of gods who presided over the **geysers** and thermal springs in the region of Palakia in Sicily, Italy. The ancient Roman civilization used geothermal water at Pompeii, Italy, to heat buildings. Medieval wars were fought over lands that contained hot springs.

core: the innermost layer of the earth, made of solid and liquid iron.

mantle: the middle layer of the earth between the crust and the core.

crust: the outer, thin layer of the earth.

WORDS TO KNOW

The world's oldest geothermal district heating system is in France, where it has been operating since the fourteenth century.

In 1892, America's first geothermal energy heating system powered Boise, Idaho. The first geothermal plant to generate electricity was built in 1921. There are now 17 geothermal heating systems in the United States and dozens more around the world. Today, homes and dwellings are still built near springs to take advantage of the natural heat of these geothermal springs.

How do we find all this geothermal power? The earth, just like humans and animals, has interacting parts.

On the Surface

We don't need to drill deep into the earth to tap into geothermal energy. In fact, geothermal energy is released right at the surface of the earth in many places. Volcanoes are areas where the geothermal energy is escaping. Lava is rock that has melted and flows out of volcanoes. Hot springs are natural pools of water that have been warmed by the heat of the earth. You can see all the places in the world where volcanoes are present on this map.

volcano discovery map 🔍

This map shows areas where hot springs are found in the United States. Do you notice anything about the areas that have the most hot springs?

NOAA hot springs map 🔍

Imagine cutting the earth in half just as you might cut an apple. You would see three distinct layers of the planet. The **core**, the **mantle**, and the **crust**. These layers vary in thickness.

How thick is the skin of an apple? It is barely the width of a piece of paper! Similarly, the skin of the earth, also called the earth's crust, is paper thin when compared to the immense thickness of the earth. The crust is 0.0004 (4 ten-thousandths) the thickness of the earth. Where do you think the earth's crust is thickest? Where do you think it is thinnest?

The earth's crust varies from mountaintops to the ocean floor. The thicker parts of crust or continental crust, are near mountains, such as the Himalayan and Andes Mountains. Here, the crust can be up to 40 miles thick. The thinnest parts of the crust are found under the ocean and are called oceanic crust. Many places on the ocean floor have a crust that is only 3 miles thick. That is about 352 schools buses lined up.

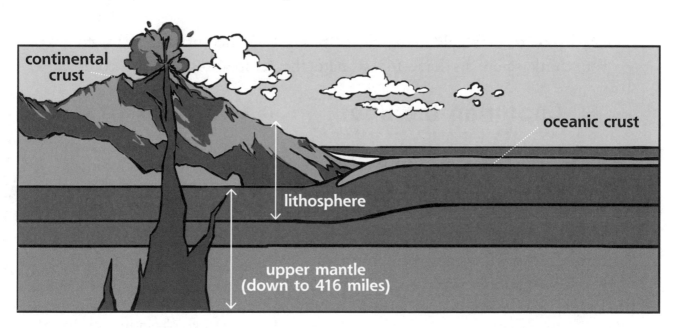

continental crust

oceanic crust

lithosphere

upper mantle
(down to 416 miles)

seismic waves: a form of energy released by earthquakes.

estimate: to form a general idea about the value, size, or cost of something.

lithosphere: the outer part of the earth, consisting of the crust and upper mantle.

piston: a sliding piece that moves up and down or back and forth.

geothermal heat pump: a system used to get energy from below the surface of the earth.

WORDS TO KNOW

Thanks to earthquakes and the **seismic waves** they give off, we can gather data about the inside of the earth. This data tells us about our planet's inner temperatures and the thickness of the layers inside the earth. The seismic data shows that the earth's inner and outer cores are about 2,100 miles thick. That is equal to 246,000 school buses lined up. The earth's mantle is 1,800 miles thick.

The deeper you go into the earth, the hotter the temperatures.

At the very center of the earth, in the inner core, scientists **estimate** that the temperature is more than 10,000 degrees Fahrenheit. That is hot enough to melt solid iron! The mantle is also very hot, hotter than the surface of Venus. The crust of the earth, also called the **lithosphere**, gets colder the closer you get to the surface. Why do you think scientists have to estimate the temperature in the core?

Capturing the Heat

As you have learned in previous chapters, energy is converted into electricity by getting a magnet inside a turbine to spin. How does geothermal energy get a turbine to spin? Simply by using steam. Just as steam powered trains in the 1800s, steam from geothermal is now powering cities.

Plugged In

Scientists believe Mars, Venus, Mercury, and our own moon all once had superheated cores similar to the earth. Ancient volcanoes on Venus and Mars point to this. In fact, Mars has the largest volcano in the solar system, called Olympus Mons. Earth, as far as we know, is the only rocky planet that still has a super-hot, liquid core.

Steam engine

Geothermal system

In a steam engine, the conductor burns coal to heat water. As the water boils, it changes from a liquid to a gas, or steam. When forced into the engine of the train, the steam causes the engine to move. The **piston's** movements cause the wheels of the train to spin.

With geothermal energy, there is no need to burn fossil fuels to create steam. Instead, the hot rocks are used to change liquid water into steam. The steam's movement causes the blades of a turbine to spin and generate electricity. Hot stuff!

GREEN JOBS

Geothermal Technicians

Geothermal technicians are the experts you need at a geothermal power plant. These people help monitor, control, and repair the devices that harness the geothermal power. Many of them help maintain **geothermal heat pumps** used to create electricity from geothermal energy.

Plugged In

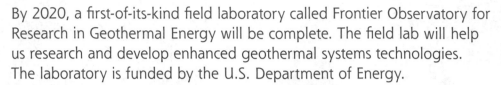

By 2020, a first-of-its-kind field laboratory called Frontier Observatory for Research in Geothermal Energy will be complete. The field lab will help us research and develop enhanced geothermal systems technologies. The laboratory is funded by the U.S. Department of Energy.

Scientists and engineers have also figured out how to use certain properties of the earth's crust to heat and cool homes and businesses. Although many parts of the country experience seasonal temperature extremes, from scorching heat in the summer to sub-zero cold in the winter, a few feet below the earth's surface, the ground remains at a relatively constant temperature. This is why animals burrow underground in the winter—they're searching for a cozy spot.

Finding That Heat

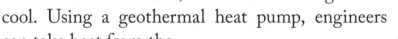

We might not always feel it, but the surface of the earth is always releasing or holding heat. That means that in the winter, when it is cold outside, a few feet underground it remains warm. In the summer, when it is hot outside, a few feet underground it is cool. Using a geothermal heat pump, engineers can take heat from the ground in winter to help heat your house.

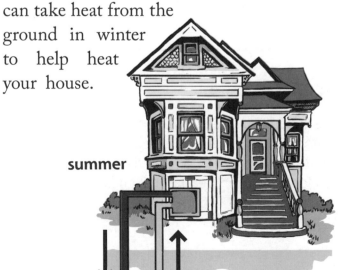

summer

winter

In the summer, the cool temperature underground can be used to help cool your house. Some geothermal heat pumps are even able to supply a home with hot water for cooking and bathing.

Geothermal energy experts drill into the earth's crust with very big drills to find areas with the hottest temperatures.

Have you ever seen a home power drill? How long is the longest drill bit? Most power drills have a drill bit that is at most a few inches long. Geothermal scientists use drills that are miles long. In fact, the deepest scientists have ever drilled into the earth is 40,230 feet or 7.62 miles. That's a long drill bit!

There are lots of places where the earth's geothermal energy is at work. In Iceland, much of the country runs on geothermal energy. The tiny island of Martinique, in the Caribbean, is currently drilling wells to power the community on geothermal energy.

GREEN JOBS

Geothermal Scientist

Do you dig earth science? Earth science rocks! Jobs in research and development of geothermal technology may be the right fit for you. These jobs in industry, national labs, and universities provide data and analysis to help us understand the power within the earth. Maybe you can help us locate that geothermal energy.

The nation of Costa Rica recently celebrated 100 days of running on 100 percent renewable energies. Costa Rica uses large quantities of geothermal energy.

The United States remains a leader in geothermal energy production and has vast geothermal energy potential just waiting for the next **geologist** explorer. The first large-scale geothermal power plant went live in 1960. Today, the United States powers more than 3.5 million homes with clean, renewable, geothermal energy.

Plugged In

Venus and Mars once had magnetospheres, but as their cores cooled the magnetospheres disappeared.

The core of the earth produces our **magnetosphere**, which protects us from some of the sun's cosmic rays. The heat from the core of the earth causes earthquakes, creates volcanoes, and can even move mountains. Inside your body beats a heart that's pumping blood, which provides your entire body with the nutrients and oxygen required for life. Similarly, the core of the earth creates heat just like the heart pumps blood.

Geopower

Geothermal energy is a clean energy that is safe to use. Watch this video highlighting the basic principles at work in geothermal energy. The video illustrates three different ways the earth's heat can be converted into electricity.

> department of energy geothermal video 🔍

Take a look at this map showing areas in the United States where the temperatures of the rocks are warmer and cooler. Which region has the greatest potential?

> interactive geothermal map 🔍

ENERGY TRADE-OFFS

Geothermal Energy Trade-offs

Geothermal energy can produce a predictable, constant flow of energy. The problem with geothermal energy is the high cost of digging deep into the earth. It costs millions of dollars to drill a single geothermal energy well. Geologists are working hard to help us identify geothermal sources to power our lives. But it is hard to be 100 percent right when finding that heat for use. Sometimes, a geothermal well is drilled that does not have enough heat to produce energy. This is a risky proposition for any business person.

The super-hot core provides us with a chance to generate clean, renewable energy. This can support our society's demand for electricity without polluting. Geothermal is a strong renewable energy Olympic competitor because it can produce a steady source of electricity 24 hours a day without interruption.

The more you learn, the more you realize that the earth's ability to provide us with clean, renewable energy is amazing. There has been steady continued growth in geothermal energy use since the 1970s.

How far can we go using this renewable energy? That is up to the next generation of geothermal engineers. We have one more renewable energy technology to explore. Buckle up, because this energy just might change how we power our cars.

ESSENTIAL QUESTION

Now it's time to consider and discuss the Essential Question: What is geothermal energy and how can we make it useful?

HOT LAVA

IDEAS FOR SUPPLIES

newspaper • bowl • measuring cups • sand • baking soda
red food coloring • paper cup • vinegar • hot water • safety goggles

Volcanoes are found everywhere on our planet. These are places where geothermal energy from deep inside the earth comes to the surface. You can create your own volcano.

Caution: This project is messy so make sure to cover your work surface or do the experiment outside. You should also wear safety goggles.

1 Cover a large work surface with plenty of newspaper.

2 In a bowl, mix ½ cup sand with ½ cup baking soda. Add red food coloring and mix well. This will be your lava. Put the lava mixture into the paper cup. The cup will be the crater of your volcano. Clean out the bowl.

3 Pour a pile of sand onto the newspaper and get it slightly wet. The sand needs to be moist enough to stick together. Mound the sand around the paper cup to create the outside of your volcano. The top of the cup is the crater and you should leave it open.

4 Put on the safety goggles. In the clean bowl, mix ½ cup hot water with ½ cup vinegar. Slowly, pour the liquid mixture from the bowl into the crater. Stand back and watch what happens.

THINK ABOUT IT: When a real volcano erupts, what is the lava made of? As it cools after an eruption, what does it become?

CROSS SECTION OF THE EARTH

IDEAS FOR SUPPLIES
6 different colors of clay • *plastic knife*

Geothermal energy starts from deep inside the earth. Then it slowly makes its way to the surface. In this activity, you will learn the parts of the earth by making a model of the earth out of clay.

1 Make a small ball from the yellow clay to represent the earth's inner core. Cover the ball with layers of red, orange, and brown clay. These represent the layers of the earth. Read back through the chapter to find how thick they should be.

2 Use green and blue clay to cover the earth. These colors represent the water and land.

3 Once your earth is whole, cut into it to make a cross section. Observe your cross section of the earth. Try to identify three areas where the crust is thinnest. These might represent the best places for geothermal power plants to be placed. Make a drawing of your model in your science journal and label the parts of the earth.

TRY THIS: Choose three different kinds of fruit, such as an apple, peach, and orange. Predict which fruit will have structures most like that of the earth. With the help of an adult, cut each fruit in half. How thick are the parts of the fruit? Use a ruler to measure the different thicknesses and compare them to each other. Which one is most like the earth?

ACTIVITY

GEOTHERMAL STEAM POWER PLANT

IDEAS FOR SUPPLIES

work gloves • empty soup can • can opener • stiff wire or coat hanger • pliers with wire cutter • duct tape • scissors • 2 aluminum pie pans • cork • thumbtack or pin • medium cooking pot • aluminum foil • hot plate or stove

How can the thermal energy in steam be converted to mechanical energy? In a geothermal power plant, steam from water heated deep underground is used to turn a turbine. This activity will help you investigate.

Caution: This activity must be done with the supervision of an adult. Be careful of sharp edges.

1 Wearing work gloves for safety, poke one hole in the bottom of the empty soup can using a can opener punch. This end will be the top, where the steam exits.

2 Cut a piece of wire and duct tape it firmly to the side of the can opposite the hole. Bend the wire so that it hangs above the hole where the steam will exit.

3 Use scissors to cut a turbine with blades from one of the aluminum pie pans. You want to make the turbine smaller in diameter than the can.

4 Push the cork onto the end of the wire. Use a thumbtack or pin to attach the center of the turbine to the center of the cork suspended over the can. The turbine should hang horizontally and spin freely.

WORDS TO KNOW

mechanical energy: energy that uses physical parts you can see, such as the parts of a machine. It is related to motion and height.

ACTIVITY

5 Fill a medium pot halfway with water and cap it with a secure layer of aluminum foil. Be sure to wrap the edges under the lip of the pan to minimize steam escape.

6 Poke a hole about half the diameter of the soup can in the middle of the foil.

7 Cut a hole in the center of the other aluminum pie pan the same diameter as the hole in the foil. Place this pie plate directly on top of the foil. This will provide support for the soup can and turbine.

8 Now place the soup can and turbine assembly directly over the holes in the tin foil and the pie plate. With an adult's help, boil the water to create steam and record your observations.

TRY THIS: Experiment with different sizes and configurations of holes for the steam to pass through. Consider building a second or third design for your turbine blades. How do changes in the angle or the diameter of the turbine change your results? The speed of the turbine can be calculated by putting a mark on one edge of the turbine and counting how many revolutions it makes in a specific amount of time. This will help you to compare your designs.

THERMAL AND MECHANICAL ENERGY

IDEAS FOR SUPPLIES
paper clips • *rubber band*

This activity is a series of small experiments and observations to help you learn more about the different types of energy.

1 Put your hands on your cheeks. Notice how your hands feel. Write down your observation in your science journal.

2 Now rub your hands together rapidly for 10 seconds. Place your hands back on your cheeks. Write down your observations in your science journal.

3 Now pick up a paper clip. Can you think of how you would show the same energy transformations with a paper clip? Write down your ideas in your science journal. Test it out with the paper clip by bending it back and forth 10 times. Feel the location of the clip where the bending is taking place.

4 Next grab a rubber band. Hold it firmly with your index fingers inside the ends of the rubber band and your thumbs on the outside. Place the rubber band flat against your forehead.

5 While keeping it against your forehead, stretch the rubber band to twice its original length. Hold for three seconds. Repeat three times. Write down your observations. What types of energy did you observe?

TRY THIS: The inside of a car's engine produces both thermal and mechanical energy. Ask a parent to lift the hood on your family car after your next long road trip and see what you can observe.

Chapter 5

CIRCLE OF LIFE

What do wind, solar, and water power all share? They all rely on energy from the sun. There is one more renewable energy source that is also powered by the sun—bioenergy, which is generated from biomass.

So far, most of what we have learned about renewable sources has been focused on how we make electricity. Remember, we use a lot of electricity! What else do we need power for that requires a lot of energy? Transportation.

? ESSENTIAL QUESTION

Why does biofuel make sense as an alternative to gasoline?

WORDS TO KNOW

bioenergy: energy contained in living or recently living things.

organic matter: decaying plants and animals.

convert: to change a material into something else.

herbaceous: having characteristics of a plant with a non-woody stem.

ethanol: a colorless, flammable liquid.

biodiesel: a fuel from vegetable sources.

biogas: a gas made from something that was once alive.

International Space Station

We move goods and people all around the world. From cars and airplanes to ships and trains, almost all these vehicles use fossil fuels.

Each day, the world burns 3,900,000,000 gallons of oil. If we stacked this oil in gallon milk jug containers, it would be a line of milk jugs 6,164 miles long. This means that, every four days, we consume enough oil to make a solid line of gallon oil jugs around the equator of the earth, or 24,000 miles. In a little more than one month, we burn enough oil to stack our jugs to the moon, 230,000 miles away.

In just one day, we burn enough oil to stack gallon jugs to the International Space Station 25 times.

That is a lot of fossil fuels being burned! And all that burning produces a lot of greenhouse gases, including carbon dioxide (CO_2). Where does the CO_2 go? It is released into the atmosphere.

There are other types of fuels we could be using. **Bioenergy** is a renewable energy source that can be crushed, pressed, and squeezed into a renewable liquid fuel. This fuel can power our cars and help us travel the world. Let's explore how **organic matter** can replace fossil fuels in powering our transportation sector. It can even replace plastic products.

Fueling Life

Bioenergy can come in different forms, including solid, liquid, and gas. We **convert** woody plants into solid biomass. We press and squeeze **herbaceous** plants and algae into liquid

Plugged In

Eating five apples is like eating a stick of dynamite! That is because five apples have the same amount of energy—measured in calories—as one stick of dynamite. One apple has 108 calories and one stick of dynamite has 504 calories. One gallon of gasoline has 31,500 calories.

biofuels, such as **ethanol** and **biodiesel**. We can even take food grease, animal waste, and garbage and convert them into usable forms of energy called **biogas**, or methane.

All these varieties of biofuels come from the energy stored in the organic matter in plants.

All animals, including humans, use bioenergy. The energy in food powers our bodies' daily activities. We measure food energy in kilocalories, which we usually just call calories. Doctors recommend that the average child between the ages of 4 and 8 years old eat 1,200 to 1,800 calories per day. The average child between 9 and 12 needs 1,600 to 2,200 calories per day. Doctors recommend adults eat around 2,000 calories a day, but the amount of calories you need depends on your weight and activity level.

WORDS TO KNOW

cell: the functional unit of an organism.

glucose: a type of sugar commonly found in plants.

photosynthesis: the process of converting the sun's energy into food in plants.

organism: any living thing.

How do we get energy out of our food? Every cell in the human body, whether it's a muscle cell, brain cell, or heart cell, needs energy to work. This energy comes from the food we eat. We digest the food we eat by mixing it with our stomach fluids. This process breaks down the food into smaller and smaller pieces.

When the stomach digests food, the food breaks down into a simple sugar called glucose. Glucose is the energy that powers our cells. The intestines absorb glucose and then release it into our bloodstream. Once in the bloodstream, glucose can be used immediately.

Plants also need glucose. They use the process of photosynthesis to get this energy. During photosynthesis, light energy from the sun is used to turn carbon dioxide and water into glucose. The waste product from this process is oxygen, which is what we breathe.

Food going into body

Glucose powers our body

Food being digested

Bioenergy engineers convert the sugars found in plants into usable energy—biofuel! They are experts in biology, chemistry, and engineering. We can use this biofuel to power cars, trucks, trains, and planes.

Types of Bioenergy

A plant's biomass can be converted into different forms of energy, including solid biomass and liquid biofuel. Wood is the oldest form of solid biomass. Wood was the main source of energy in the world until the mid-1800s. Today, nearly 2.6 billion people still use wood for cooking and heating.

We also use other forms of solid biomass to power electrical plants. This solid biomass is made from materials such as wood, sawdust, and crop waste. These are often processed into briquettes, pellets, and charcoal.

In 1986, Barre Town Middle and Elementary School in Barre, Vermont, decided to install a wood chip boiler to heat their school. This project has saved the school millions of dollars. Now, students at the school help manage an 88-acre piece of land owned by the town that is used to provide wood chips for the school.

Green Schools

The Fuel for Schools program began in Vermont in the 1980s. This program helps schools use biomass to save on energy bills. The program expanded in 2001 through the U.S. Department of Agriculture Forest Service. Today, schools from Idaho to Vermont are saving money by using biomass!

Biologists and engineers are working to find new ways to convert the energy in biological organisms into liquid biofuels. Different plants, such as corn stover, switchgrass, sugar cane, sugar beets, and even algae can be pressed and transformed into a liquid fuel called a biofuel.

In 2013, biofuels helped provide about 5 percent of the energy in the United States.

fermentation: a chemical reaction that breaks down food and other organic matter. The process converts sugar to acids.

WORDS TO KNOW

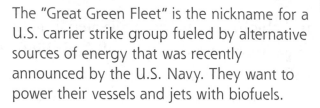

Plugged In

The "Great Green Fleet" is the nickname for a U.S. carrier strike group fueled by alternative sources of energy that was recently announced by the U.S. Navy. They want to power their vessels and jets with biofuels.

Today, biofuels are already powering cars and trucks on every road in the United States. Biofuels are providing a cleaner and more sustainable transportation system.

Ethanol

Have you ever seen an E85 symbol at a gas station? This is the symbol of a fuel blend of 85 percent ethanol. In the United States, almost all cars are running on a little bit of corn energy. That is because almost all gas stations in this country use a gasoline mixture that contains 10 percent ethanol. These cars are considered E10.

Flexible-fuel vehicles can use 85 percent ethanol, or E85. To determine if your vehicle runs on E85, check the gas cap. If your car runs on E85, the gas cap will be yellow, like the sun. Next time your family goes to the gas station, see if you can find a flex-fuel pump that has E85.

Biofuels Processing Technician

Biofuels processing technicians are the experts you need to help with **fermentation**. These experimenters are the people who help us calculate, mix, and monitor what happens with different uses of biomass. A key part of their job is to keep records and stay safe. These are the people who help make E10 and E85. What will they create next?

Ethanol is the most widely used biofuel in the world. We can make ethanol from almost any plant. Some plants, however, are better than others. In Brazil, they use sugar cane to make ethanol. In France, they use sugar beets and wheat. In the United States, we use mostly corn. Each plant produces a different amount of ethanol per acre of farmland used. The chart on the next page will show you how much this can vary.

Crops that produce more gallons per acre are more efficient.

Biodiesel is another type of renewable liquid fuel. Diesel and biodiesel can be used to power diesel engines. There are lots of different plants that can be used to create biodiesel.

Soybeans are used to create biodiesel in the United States and in Brazil. Head over to Europe, and the biodiesel comes from rapeseed. Biodiesel from jatropha, a common weed, is an increasingly popular source of energy in Haiti.

urea: a waste product made by animal cells.

biodegradable: something that can break down or decay and become absorbed into the environment.

WORDS TO KNOW

Choose the Crop

Which crop would you use if you had to choose the energy crop for your city? Why?

Ethanol and Biodiesel Yield per Acre from Selected Crops		
Crop	**Fuel**	**Fuel Yield (Gallons)**
Sugar beet (France)	Ethanol	714
Sugarcane (Brazil)	Ethanol	662
Cassava (Nigeria)	Ethanol	410
Sweet Sorghum (India)	Ethanol	374
Corn (U.S.)	Ethanol	354
Wheat (France)	Ethanol	277
Oil palm	Biodiesel	508
Coconut	Biodiesel	230
Rapeseed	Biodiesel	102
Peanut	Biodiesel	90
Sunflower	Biodiesel	82
Soybean	Biodiesel	57

What Smells?

We even can make biofuels from animal waste and our own garbage. Large pig and cow farms produce a lot of animal waste, such as manure and **urea**. By capturing animal waste and turning it into biofuels, farmers can reduce the greenhouse gases that are emitted into the atmosphere.

This reduces water and air pollution. Plus, if farmers can create their own fuel from animal manure, they don't need to purchase and use more fossil fuels.

Plugged In

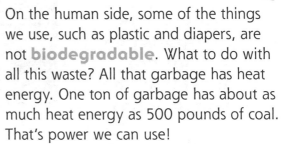

On the human side, some of the things we use, such as plastic and diapers, are not **biodegradable**. What to do with all this waste? All that garbage has heat energy. One ton of garbage has about as much heat energy as 500 pounds of coal. That's power we can use!

Some organic materials can decay with the help of bacteria. When organic matter decays, it produces methane. There are landfills across the country emitting methane into the atmosphere. Don't forget that methane is a greenhouse gas! At many landfills, engineers are creating ways to capture and utilize that methane gas. We can use methane from landfills to heat our homes and power our lights. India is currently converting cow manure into methane gas to produce electricity.

Another type of garbage that can be turned into biofuel is fast-food grease. Animal fats, greases, and vegetable oils can be mixed with alcohol to create biodiesel. In the United States alone, there are 50,000 fast-food restaurants, and in the world there are more than 500,000. Imagine if we could use their waste to create diesel for our cars.

bioproducts: fuels, chemicals, and raw materials made from renewable resources.

forest residue: what's left on the forest floor after timber has been harvested.

WORDS TO KNOW

Alternative transportation fuels are growing in the United States.

Everything we throw away took energy to make. Many types of waste, from garbage to manure to palm tree leaves and grass clippings, can be used to generate renewable energy.

There are many different ways to create biofuels from all these different types of plants. The process takes place in biorefineries.

One process for converting plants to fuel is called fermentation. Have you ever opened your refrigerator and smelled something really bad? That is a sign that fermentation has occurred. It is usually the process of something going sour. In biorefineries, we want things to go sour. Technicians cause this by using yeast and mixing it with the starch from plants.

Waste-to-energy power plants are helping us utilize our waste and become more efficient. They take advantage of the things we normally consider waste and turn them into things we can use. This helps us to make a smaller impact on the planet.

Plastic Plants

Did you know that many of your common household items are also made from fossil fuels? That is because plastics are made from fossil fuels. Plastic water bottles are one example. In the United States, we use nearly 17 million barrels of oil a year to make disposable water bottles. How many water bottles is that? In the United States, we threw away 50 billion water bottles last year. What if plastics could be made from biofuel?

GREEN JOBS

Bioprocess Engineers

Bioprocess engineers are leaders in helping create new chemicals and products. They use a lot of math, chemistry, and biology to help design and develop products from biological material.

We also use petroleum in our clothes and in printer ink. In one year, nearly 942 million ink cartridges—almost 30 cartridges per second—are sold for personal printers. That is enough ink to print 39,000,000 family pictures.

What other things do you use that are made from plastic? Could we make these things without using fossil fuels? New bioproducts are being invented every day. Using crops, wastes, grasses, and forest residues, we can create new green chemicals, paper, and additives to help us make bioproducts.

We can replace all that petroleum and still have the things we love. Take a look around your kitchen. What could be biobased? How about soaps, plates, and napkins?

Biofuels can be solid, liquid, or gas and they can come from living plants, dead plants, or even your own garbage. The future for biofuels in the United States and the world is very bright when you consider that 99.8 percent of all engines in the world still run on fossil fuels. Bioenergy is yet another competitor that relies heavily on solar energy to compete in the renewable energy Olympics. Do you rely on the sun as much as these competitors?

Plugged In

Recycling is important! Two thousands pounds of recycled paper saves up to 17 trees and uses 50 percent less water.

Maybe you want to be the next bioengineer to help create a more renewable future. Before you make that decision, let's read our final chapter to explore the communities that are making wise energy choices and leading the way in the clean energy revolution.

Algae

Scientists are investigating ways to turn algae into biofuel. Algae are aquatic organisms living in ponds, lakes, oceans, and even in wastewater. Algae use carbon dioxide to grow, which helps remove that greenhouse gas from the atmosphere. It also might be able to provide a new type of biofuel. Estimates indicate that algae can produce 60 times more biofuel per acre than land-based plants.

? ESSENTIAL QUESTION

Now it's time to consider and discuss the Essential Question:
Why does biofuel make sense as an alternative to gasoline?

Bioenergy Trade-offs

Bioenergy is probably the renewable energy source with the most trade-offs. It requires a lot of processing to create liquid or dried fuel. In addition, burning biomass does release some carbon dioxide and other pollutants into the air. That makes bioenergy the only renewable energy source that releases significant quantities of CO_2, a known greenhouse gas. Despite this, bioenergy is still preferable to fossil fuel use.

Growing and harvesting biomass requires the use of fuel. Tractors, trucks, fertilizer, and farmland are used, which contributes to the release of more carbon dioxide. Bioenergy can also consume large quantities of water, whether it's to grow crops for solid fuels or algae for liquid fuels.

These trade-offs are considerable, but we are discovering new ways to turn our agricultural waste into fuel. The United States is a leader in growing corn. More than 90 million acres of land are used to grow corn. What do farmers do with the corn husks? These husks can be turned into biofuel.

Wood is an abundant bioenergy source found in our forests. Foresters and firefighters often burn fallen trees and other debris to help prevent massive forest fires. What if we could turn this waste into electricity for our homes instead? Finding methods to convert our waste to energy is important.

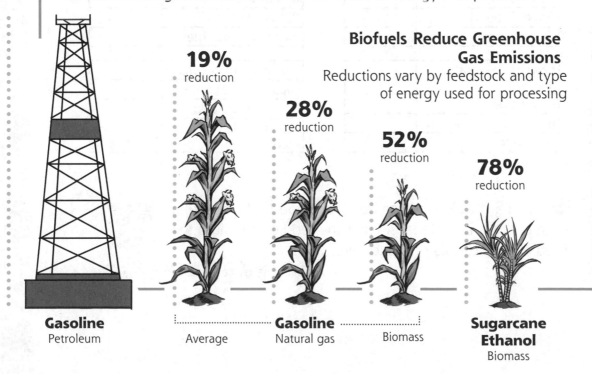

Biofuels Reduce Greenhouse Gas Emissions
Reductions vary by feedstock and type of energy used for processing

19% reduction

28% reduction

52% reduction

78% reduction

Gasoline
Petroleum

Average

Gasoline
Natural gas

Biomass

Sugarcane Ethanol
Biomass

FOOD HAS ENERGY

What provides your body with energy? Food! Food energy is the amount of energy in food when it is digested. This energy is measured in calories.

1 In your science journal, record everything you eat for an entire day. This food is where you get the energy to go to school and to do all of the activities you love.

2 Start an Energy in Your Food worksheet like the one here, using all of the foods you ate. Rank the foods from least (1) to most (4) energy you think you can get from that food.

For each group, rank the foods (1–4) by the amounts of energy you think they contain (1=least, 4=most).

cheeseburger	
plain hot dog on bun	
6 chicken nuggets	
small taco	

milk	
soda	
orange juice	
water	

banana	
large carrot	
cup of broccoli	
slice of cheese	

slice of pepperoni pizza	
nachos with cheese	
PBJ sandwich	
medium French fries	

bowl of Cheerios and milk	
granola bar	
6 chicken nuggets	
small taco	

2 peanut butter cups	
cup of ice cream	
bag of potato chips	
cup of sunflower seeds	

3 With an adult, estimate how many food calories are in each of your ranked foods. Enter the food calories into the food energy calculator found here.

food energy calculator for kids 🔍

4 In your journal write down which food provides you with the most energy. How did your original prediction compare to what you found using the energy calculator?

5 Use the picture below to label where on your body the activities occur. Add to your picture how many calories you think you use to complete that activity.

- **running**
- **crunches**
- **hiking**
- **soccer**
- **hula hooping**
- **volleyball**
- **dancing**
- **touch football**
- **kickball**
- **yoga**

6 Which activity requires the most energy and which requires the least energy? Remember, you consume about 2,000 calories a day.

activity calorie calculator for kids 🔍

POTATO POWER

IDEAS FOR SUPPLIES

potato • knife • paper plate • 2 galvanized nails • 2 pennies •
3 pieces of 8-inch insulated copper wire • miniature light bulb

**In this experiment, the energy comes from the
reaction between the metals, and the potato acts
as a buffer for the energy to pass through.**

Caution: Ask an adult to help with the knife.

1 Cut the potato in half with the knife. Put the halves cut-side down on the paper plate.

2 Wrap one piece of copper wire around one of the nails. Wrap a second piece of wire around one of the pennies. Make sure both wire ends are left loose each time. Push the penny and the nail into the same potato half, but make sure they do not touch.

3 Wrap the third piece of wire around the second penny in the same way. Push the penny into the other potato half. Put the second nail into the second potato half. This nail should not have any wire on it.

4 Time to make the connection! Connect the penny in the first potato to the nail in the second.

5 Connect the two other pieces of wire to the two wires coming off of a miniature light bulb or use old holiday lights and cut off one light bulb. What happens to the light bulb? Why?

Nuclear Energy: Renewable?

There are two types of nuclear energy—nuclear fission and nuclear fusion. We have been harnessing electricity from nuclear fission for decades and it is the largest source of carbon-free electricity in the United States. At nuclear power plants, the heat to make the steam needed to generate electricity is created when atoms split apart. This is called fission. It releases energy in the form of heat. In most cases, the fuel used for nuclear fission is uranium. Unlike solar power and wind energy, uranium is a non-renewable resource, which is why fission is not considered renewable energy. In addition, fission produces radioactive waste that is highly dangerous to human health and must be stored in special containers for thousands of years.

Nuclear fusion involves joining the nuclei from two atoms to make a larger nucleus, a reaction that also releases energy. The energy released by the sun and other stars is created by the process of nuclear fusion. The sequence of nuclear fusion reactions in a star is complex, but basically, hydrogen nuclei join to form helium nuclei. Engineers are trying to create the same power of the sun in a laboratory using controlled nuclear fusion reactions. This technology is decades, possibly centuries, away from commercial use to generate electricity. But since this reaction relies on hydrogen, the most abundant element in the universe, many people consider this a potentially unlimited renewable energy resource.

THINK ABOUT IT: Can you power a simple motor from a hobby shop with your potato battery? Try making a simple toothbrush robot, then use the potato battery to power it. If you need more power, how can you create it?

toothbrush robot 🔍

BIODIESEL AND ETHANOL

IDEAS FOR SUPPLIES

safety goggles • resealable bag • leaves • grass clippings • leftover food • yeast • bottle of grape juice • rubbing alcohol • glass beakers • matches

In this activity, you will explore how foods in your kitchen can make fuels. Have you ever eaten a soybean? Edamame? Corn? All of these foods have been turned into biodiesel to help us fuel cars, trucks, and anything that needs gas. Let's make some biogas! This activity takes two weeks to complete.

Caution: An adult must help with this. Wear your safety glasses.

1 Fill a resealable bag with leaves and grass clippings, leftovers from lunch, and a pinch of yeast. Add a little water, if necessary, so that the mixture is moist.

2 Force out as much air as possible by flattening the bag before closing. Put the bag in a warm place. Watch it for a week. What happens to the bag? Record your observations in your science journal.

3 Open the bottle of grape juice and add a pinch of yeast. Recap the bottle and set it on a windowsill near the bag of leaves and leftovers to allow fermentation to occur. The juice and yeast mixture will turn into alcohol. How? The yeast eats the sugar in the grape juice, releasing both CO_2 and alcohol.

4 After two weeks, smell the juice. How can the alcohol in the grape juice and the bag of biogas be used for fuel? Write down your ideas in your science journal.

TRY THIS: With the help of an adult, experiment with the biogas to learn how alcohol can burn. Get two glass beakers. Pour some rubbing alcohol in one and your biogas mixture in the other. Put on your safety goggles! With an adult, use matches to light the liquid in each glass beaker. This will show you how alcohol can be burned as a fuel.

ENERGIZING OUR FUTURE

From the core of the earth to the surface of the sun, which floats 93,000,000 miles away, there are many renewable sources to power our world. Are any of them better than the others?

Our world will need all these technologies to work as a team to replace fossil fuels. There is one more thing this team will need—us! The future of our planet and our communities are defined by our energy choices of today.

? ESSENTIAL QUESTION

Which renewable energy is the best choice for these different uses: Fueling cars, heating homes, producing electricity, warming water, and powering factories?

survey: to examine or measure something.

WORDS TO KNOW

Researching the Future

New inventions and advances in renewable technologies will change our energy future. How much electricity do you use every day? From flipping a light switch to powering your MP3 player to storing cold food, we all need electricity. But burning fossil fuels pollutes our air and water and damages the health of our planet. Burning fossil fuels causes global warming and climate change. Using renewable energy sources is part of the solution. Renewable energy will help us create a healthier future and provide electricity to more people.

The U.S. Department of Energy has 17 national laboratories. These laboratories make up the largest scientific research system in the world. Department of Energy geologists work to **survey** the land to find the best locations for wind and geothermal power. Meanwhile, scientists at the labs focus on research and development projects that will make renewable technologies more efficient.

The work that happens within these labs is helping to lead the way in creating a more renewable future energy economy.

Every day, engineers work to improve the absorption of solar cells, redesign wind turbine blades, and improve hydropower plants.

Improving Energy Efficiency

What does it mean to be more efficient? What do you do to make yourself more efficient in your schoolwork, homework, and sports?

Energy efficiency means trying to capture more energy and waste less. Anytime we capture or use energy, there is waste. Being efficient means that we use processes or materials that reduce the amount of wasted energy.

A solar panel is an excellent example of how efficiency can improve. In the 1970s, a solar panel could capture between 4 and 6 percent of the energy that struck its surface. That meant 96 percent of the energy was lost as heat. In 2015, a high-efficiency research solar panel can capture as much as 40 percent of the energy that strikes its surface.

Plugged In

There are nearly 1.3 billion people in the world without access to electricity. What do they use instead? They use other sources for heat and light, such as wood, candles, and oil lamps.

The efficiency of solar panels has increased quite dramatically through research and new designs. In addition, the amount of material used in a 1-meter solar panel has decreased. Engineers are now more efficient when they build solar panels as well.

What about the lights in your house? Have you ever held your hand up close to a light bulb without touching it? What did you feel? An incandescent light bulb wastes 90 percent

Incandescent

of the energy it uses. While generating light, it generates lots of heat! This heat is wasted. How many light bulbs do you have in your house? Turning off just one 60-watt incandescent bulb can help reduce carbon dioxide and lower your electricity bill. Turning off one 60-watt light bulb that normally is on eight hours a day saves 1,000 pounds of carbon dioxide over the lifetime of that bulb.

Compact fluorescent (CFL)

Incandescent bulbs are not efficient. Are there alternatives?

Halogen

Light bulbs are changing in terms of their efficiency and in the design of the bulbs. Now we have a choice about the type of light bulb we use. We can install halogen, compact fluorescent, or light-emitting diodes (LEDs). Halogen light bulbs last nearly three times longer than incandescent light bulbs. Compact fluorescent lights last 10 times longer!

LEDs are new, super-efficient light bulbs. These are 90 percent efficient, which means they lose only 10 percent of the energy they use. While LEDs use less energy, they also last about 25 times longer than incandescent bulbs and provide more light. Choosing more energy-efficient light bulbs is an easy way to get started saving energy.

Light-emitting diode (LED)

How do we know if a gasoline-powered car is efficient? We measure that with miles per gallon.

This measurement tells you how many miles you can go on one gallon of gas. A car that can go 40 miles with one gallon is really efficient!

Today, the average fuel efficiency of a car is 24.6 miles for every gallon of gasoline. The federal government has set a new efficiency standard for 2025. By the year 2025, all cars need to have an average fuel efficiency of 54.6 miles per gallon. That means efficiency has to increase more than 100 percent. It has to more than double. The new efficiency standard will save millions of gallons of gasoline from being burned and emitting CO_2.

Making cars more efficient is an important job of automakers. Each year, engineers figure out ways to make gasoline cars more efficient. They also try to improve on electric vehicles. We learned about vehicles that use biofuels, but there are other options, such as all-electric or plug-in **hybrid** electric. Both of these use electricity to power the car, but hybrid electric cars use gasoline as a back-up fuel.

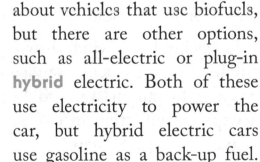

Plugged In

Henry Ford's Model T, which was produced between 1908 and 1927, got between 13 and 21 miles to the gallon.

Researchers at Argonne National Laboratory in Chicago, Illinois, are working hard to make electric and hybrid vehicles more efficient.

A 100-percent electric vehicle produces zero carbon dioxide and doesn't even have a tailpipe. The drawback is that this kind of vehicle has a limited range, usually between 70 to 100 miles, before it needs recharging.

Highway U.S. 95, which runs 445 miles in Nevada from Reno to Las Vegas, is the first electric highway in the United States. Electric charging stations are placed at regular intervals along a stretch of road, which allows electric cars to travel long distances. Just like

fossil fuel cars, electric cars can stop at a "fuel station" and recharge. The goal is to get more electric plug-in vehicles on the road, so increasing the number of charging stations is an important step.

Engineers are also working to design buildings in ways that waste less energy. Can you think of ways that a building could be more energy efficient?

Replacing leaky windows with airtight ones is one way to make a building more efficient. Newspaper insulation used to be a common material to put in walls to help keep the heat inside. Replacing newspaper insulation in old buildings with high-quality insulation is another positive step.

How about adding green space to roofs? Gardens on the tops of buildings provide great places for families and communities to share. Increasing the number of plants instead of adding more concrete helps to absorb CO_2 from the air. Green roofs also improve the insulation of a building, making them more efficient. Anything that can be done to make buildings more energy efficient saves money and reduces our CO_2 emissions.

Buildings that follow some of the best practices for protecting the environment are designated as Leadership in Energy & Environmental Design (LEED) buildings. LEED encourages people to build energy-efficient buildings. Are there LEED buildings in your community? Do some research to find out and then go visit one.

All of this research and these new designs help us be more efficient. But we need people, school officials, and business people asking for and using renewable technologies. You, too, can join the clean-energy movement by taking energy-saving actions.

Top 10 Actions to Save Energy in Your House!

- [ ] Unplug electronics, including your computer, iPod, and cell phone.
- [ ] Turn on the lights only when and where you really need them. Turn off the lights whenever you leave a room.
- [ ] Use energy-efficient light bulbs. With a parent or a family member, do some research on the best light bulbs to power your home.
- [ ] Use power strips. When you have a lot of devices to plug in, power strips help to conserve and use energy efficiently. With the flick of a switch, you can turn everything off at once.
- [ ] Shut your curtains on hot sunny days to help keep your room cool.
- [ ] Once a week, have a sandwich night for dinner instead of cooking. This saves gas and electricity.
- [ ] On a sunny day, hang your clothes outside to dry instead of using the dryer.
- [ ] Walk or use a bike instead of taking your car. Ride a bus or carpool.
- [ ] Keep the refrigerator closed. It releases a lot of energy when open.
- [ ] Reuse containers. Don't throw out that plastic container from the restaurant! Reuse it tomorrow for lunch!

Energy-Efficient Actions

How do your energy choices affect the future? Thinking about our actions is important for our clean future. It's not just researchers, engineers, and inventors helping to make renewable technology more efficient. There are actions we can take in our homes, schools, and businesses to waste less energy. To use less energy is to conserve energy.

Do you leave your game console and cell phone plugged in all night long? Do you leave the lights on in your bedroom even when you're not there? Does your family drive to places that are close enough to walk to? Do you buy a lot of new things? Do you eat a lot of meat? Do you know how much energy you use in a day?

Make a list of all the actions you do in a day that require energy. You can start by thinking of actions in your home, neighborhood, and classroom. All of the energy you use that releases CO_2 makes up your carbon footprint. Now, take your list and brainstorm.

What can you do to make your energy use more efficient? What can you do to reduce your energy use?

PS Green Button Data

New devices called smart meters are allowing some homes to track their energy consumption more closely. All electricity users have meters that are used to measure how much energy they use. This metered data is used by energy service providers to calculate how much that energy will cost you. Today, some consumers are using Green Button data. Green Button makes the data available to families and helps you make smart energy choices.

green button data 🔍

STEM Jobs Go Green

Many of the renewable energy jobs require common skills. Specific areas of expertise may vary depending on the type of renewable energy. But all are important to growing and improving each individual renewable energy sector.

- Engineers design and build specific renewable technologies.

- Technicians monitor and repair the technologies that convert renewable energy into electricity, such as solar panels and wind turbines.

- Researchers ask questions and solve problems, such as improving the efficiency of solar cells.

- Project managers organize renewable energy projects and make sure they get completed.

- Geologists and biologists help us understand the natural systems of the earth and of life to find ways to extract energy for use.

Studies show that as many as one in four workers will have jobs in the renewable energy or energy efficiency fields by 2030.

Plugged In

Look for the Energy Efficiency Rating stickers on appliances. The higher the number, the more efficient the product. These labels can help your family make smart energy choices in your home.

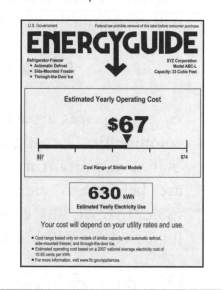

U.S. Government — Federal law prohibits removal of this label before consumer purchase.

ENERGYGUIDE

Refrigerator-Freezer
- Automatic Defrost
- Side-Mounted Freezer
- Through-the-Door Ice

XYZ Corporation
Model ABC-L
Capacity: 23 Cubic Feet

Estimated Yearly Operating Cost

$67

$57 $74

Cost Range of Similar Models

630 kWh
Estimated Yearly Electricity Use

Your cost will depend on your utility rates and use.

- Cost range based only on models of similar capacity with automatic defrost, side-mounted freezer, and through-the-door ice.
- Estimated operating cost based on a 2007 national average electricity cost of 10.65 cents per kWh.
- For more information, visit www.ftc.gov/appliances.

Building managers will need to know who to call if a solar panel breaks and they cannot fix it themselves. Factories that once created the steel nails and bolts for our railroads are creating wind turbine blades and devices for harnessing tidal wave energy.

Farming and recycling jobs are expanding into new focus areas, such as wind farming and waste-to-energy plants. Many jobs will focus on **retrofitting** old buildings and creating new green buildings! Explore all the renewable energy jobs that are available now and will be available in the future.

Clean Energy Communities

In many places around the world, renewables are already powering communities. Local governments are leading the way. In the United States, that means mayors, city councils, and even individual citizens are helping to create renewable energy partnerships. By 2014, more than 1,300 communities had worked collectively to create increased renewable energy. These collaborations, called community choice aggregation, work to increase energy choices for consumers.

Small island locations around the world are also leading the way. One island in Denmark, called Samsø, is getting 100 percent of its electricity from renewable energy.

Plugged In

The international organization Clean Energy Education & Empowerment, sometimes known as C3E, is dedicated to helping women advance in clean energy sectors. Scientists, engineers, environmental advocates, and policy leaders are part of the organization.

Samsø has nearly 4,000 people and all of its electricity comes from biomass, solar, and wind. The population has been working on using less coal since 1997. By 2030, the island will eliminate all fossil fuel use there.

Other islands, such as in Hawaii and the Caribbean, are working to lead the way by setting renewable energy goals. Hawaii declared that by 2045 it will be 100 percent reliant on renewables. Islands are important leaders in this area. They often see the first impacts of climate change and have high energy costs because fossil fuels need to come to them from long distances.

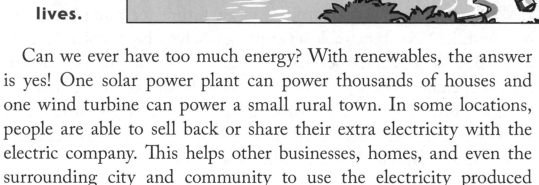

Islands are prime locations to see how renewable energy can transform lives.

Can we ever have too much energy? With renewables, the answer is yes! One solar power plant can power thousands of houses and one wind turbine can power a small rural town. In some locations, people are able to sell back or share their extra electricity with the electric company. This helps other businesses, homes, and even the surrounding city and community to use the electricity produced with renewable energy.

In 2012, the district of Rhein-Hunsruck in Frankfurt, Germany, was producing 230 percent of its energy needs. That meant it could power itself nearly two times over!

Healthy Screen Time

See how Nicaragua, one of the smallest and poorest countries in Central America, will start to export clean electricity. You can view many videos about communities that are trying to save money and be energy world leaders. Maybe you'll be inspired!

climate reality video 🔍

Instead of wasting that energy, they put it back into the national electric system.

Take a look at how some businesses are leading the way in investing and using renewable energy. Facebook, Walmart, Microsoft, Dow Chemical, and Hewlett-Packard (HP) are all buying wind power from Texas. HP, a computer manufacturer and data center company, will use wind power to help with its data center operations in the Texas area.

We have the power to make a clean future for our planet and our families. No renewable energy can solve the problem on its own. But as a team, they can change our world for the better. And remember, being outside is a critical part of the renewable energy future. What are we striving for if we don't go outside and appreciate the clean air? Play in the sunshine, the rain, and the wind, and enjoy all that the earth has to offer.

ESSENTIAL QUESTION

Now it's time to consider and discuss the Essential Question: Which renewable energy is the best choice for these different uses: fueling cars, heating homes, producing electricity, warming water, and powering factories?

CONDUCT A SCHOOL ENERGY SURVEY

Now that you know about renewable energy sources, let's go on a mission to understand how our school or classroom is using energy.

1 Use this survey to gather data.

- **What kind of energy heats our school in winter?**
- **What kind of energy cools our school in summer?**
- **What kind of energy cooks our food?**
- **What kind of energy heats our water?**
- **What kind of energy runs our school buses?**
- **What kind of energy powers our lights and our computers?**
- **What kinds of things does the school recycle?**
- **How do we waste energy?**
- **How do we save energy?**
- **What things can we do to save more energy?**

2 Brainstorm ways to help save energy in your school or classroom.

TRY THIS: Meet with your school officials to help start an energy-saving campaign. Create a school campaign with the help of your principal to save energy. Classes can compete to save the most energy.

IMAGINE A CLEAN ENERGY FUTURE

IDEAS FOR SUPPLIES

construction paper • copy paper • paper bags • tissue paper • marbled paper • magazines or newsprint • foil or colored masking tape • decorating supplies • old photographs • glue

It is important to set clean energy goals for ourselves, our communities, our country, and our world. In this activity, you can make a collage of images and words to help adults understand what type of future you wish to live in. Use this collage when talking to people about renewable energy, about clean air and clean water, or simply about your dreams for a better future.

On the back of your collage make a commitment to action by writing down three ways you will be more efficient in your use of energy. Keep in mind this statement: "We do not inherit the earth from our ancestors; we borrow it from our children."

1 Collect the materials you want to use to make a paper collage. Take some time to think about what you are trying to communicate about a sustainable future.

2 Make a list of words or phrases that you'd like to include in your collage. You can write a poem or an inspirational quote, or even tell a story. This is your chance to express how you feel about a sustainable future and the role renewable energy plays in that future.

3 Fold, cut, and tear the paper into different shapes. Make words by cutting letters from different magazines and newspapers. Find images from these sources that help you communicate your message or draw them yourself.

ACTIVITY

4 Use ribbons, beads, string, feathers, and fabric in the collage. Find these items around the house or purchase them at a craft store. Using recycled materials gives your collage extra meaning. You can also find items outside, such as colored leaves or other natural objects.

5 Assemble the pieces before you glue them. You want your collage to be visually appealing as well as to convey your message. Rearrange the pieces as necessary, then glue your collage together and let it dry.

TRY THIS: Being outside is a critical part of the renewable energy future. Play in the sunshine, the rain, and the wind, and enjoy all that the earth has to offer. Keep a journal of all the outdoor places you go to. Set a goal of one nature hike a week, and when you are done with your hike, write about what you saw, smelled, and touched, and how you felt.

CALCULATING YOUR CARBON FOOTPRINT

Understanding car fuel consumption and efficiency can help you become more informed about greenhouse gas emissions from transportation. Fossil-fuel-burning vehicles release CO_2 in the air when their motors are turned on. Knowing that the average gallon of gasoline contains about 5 pounds of carbon, calculate your "car"-bon footprint.

1 Ask your parents how many gallons of gasoline your car's (or truck's) gas tank holds. Multiply this number by five. This gives you the number of pounds of carbon your car emits every time your family empties the tank.

2 Ask your parents to reset the odometer on the car to zero next time they fill up the car. Keep track of how many miles your car goes on a full tank of gas.

3 Once the car's tank is nearly empty, record how many miles the car has gone. Divide this number by the number of gallons it takes to refill the tank. This is your miles per gallon (MPG).

4 Compare your actual MPG to the manufacturer's suggested MPG for your car. You can find this information at www.fueleconomy.gov. Is your car more or less efficient than expected? Think of at least three ways to reduce your car's carbon footprint that are related to your energy use.

THINK MORE: With permission, go online and explore actions you can take to reduce the impacts of climate change and reduce your energy use. This online interactive calculator will quiz you on activities you do, such as brushing your teeth, and help you identify ways to save energy. Take some of the simple steps and learn how your savings reduce the amount of carbon dioxide released in the air per year.

EPA climate change kid calculator 🔍

absorb: to soak up a liquid or take in energy, heat, light, or sound.

anemometer: an instrument used to measure the wind. The number of times it spins is calculated and converted into miles per hour.

archaeologist: a scientist who studies ancient people through the objects they left behind.

atmosphere: the mixture of gases surrounding a planet.

BCE: put after a date, BCE stands for Before Common Era and counts down to zero. CE stands for Common Era and counts up from zero. The year this book is published is 2016 CE.

biodegradable: something that can break down or decay and become absorbed into the environment.

biodiesel: a fuel from vegetable sources.

bioenergy: energy contained in living or recently living things.

biogas: a gas made from something that was once alive.

biomass: plant materials and animal waste used as fuel.

bioproducts: fuels, chemicals, and raw materials made from renewable resources.

byproduct: an extra and sometimes unexpected or unintended result of an action or process.

carbon: an element found in all living things.

carbon dioxide: a gas formed by the burning of fossil fuels, the rotting of plants and animals, and the breathing out of animals or humans.

carbon footprint: the total amount of carbon dioxide and other greenhouse gases emitted over the full life cycle of a product or service, or by a person, family, or community in a year.

cell: the functional unit of an organism.

climate: the average weather patterns in an area during a long period of time.

climate change: a change in the long-term average weather patterns of a place.

concentrate: to bring or direct toward the center.

condense: when a gas cools down and changes into a liquid.

conserve: to use less of something, such as energy or water.

consumption: the use of a resource.

convert: to change a material into something else.

core: the innermost layer of the earth, made of solid and liquid iron.

crust: the outer, thin layer of the earth.

dam: a wall built across a waterway to stop water flow.

data: facts about something that can be analyzed.

dense: how tightly the matter in an object is packed.

efficient: wasting as little as possible.

emissions: something that is sent or given out, such as smoke, gas, heat, or light.

engineer: a person who uses science, math, and creativity to design and build things.

engineering: the use of science and math in the design and construction of things.

equator: an imaginary line around the earth that is equally between both poles.

estimate: to form a general idea about the value, size, or cost of something.

ethanol: a colorless, flammable liquid.

evaporate: when a liquid heats up and changes into a gas.

evaporation: when the surface of a liquid changes from a liquid to a gas.

fermentation: a chemical reaction that breaks down food and other organic matter. The process converts sugar to acids.

flow: the amount of water that moves through a hydropower plant.

forest residue: what's left on the forest floor after timber has been harvested.

fossil: the remains or traces of ancient plants or animals.

fossil fuels: coal, oil, and natural gas. These energy sources come from the fossils of plants and tiny animals that lived millions of years ago.

generate: to create something or to produce energy.

geologist: a scientist who studies the solid and liquid matter that make up the earth and the forces that shape it.

geothermal: heat energy from beneath the earth's surface.

geothermal heat pump: a system used to get energy from below the surface of the earth.

geyser: a hot spring under pressure that shoots boiling water or steam into the air.

global warming: an increase in the earth's average temperatures, enough to change the climate.

glucose: a type of sugar commonly found in plants.

gravitational effect: the force of attraction between two masses.

green: something made from a renewable resource that does not harm the environment.

greenhouse gas: a gas such as water vapor, carbon dioxide, carbon monoxide, or methane that traps heat and contributes to warming temperatures.

herbaceous: having characteristics of a plant with a non-woody stem.

hot spring: a natural pool of water that is heated by hot or molten rock. Hot springs are found in areas with active volcanoes.

hybrid: a power plant, vehicle, or electronic circuit that has two different types of components performing the same function.

hydroelectric power plant: a power plant that uses moving water to power a turbine generator to produce electricity.

hydrokinetic: the motion of fluids.

hydropower: energy produced by the movement of water.

Industrial Revolution: a period of time beginning in the late 1700s when people started using machines to make things in large factories.

inexhaustible: impossible to use up completely.

innovation: a new invention or way of doing something.

irrigation: to provide water for crops through ditches, pipes, or other means.

kinetic: the movement of physical objects.

lithosphere: the outer part of the earth, consisting of the crust and upper mantle.

magnetosphere: a magnetic region surrounding an object in space.

mantle: the middle layer of the earth between the crust and the core.

manufacturing: making large quantities of products in factories using machines.

matter: what an object is made of. Anything that has weight and takes up space.

mechanical energy: energy that uses physical parts you can see, such as the parts of a machine. It is related to motion and height.

methane: a colorless, odorless greenhouse gas.

mineral: a naturally occurring solid found in rocks and in the ground. Rocks are made of minerals. Gold and diamonds are precious minerals.

observation: something you notice.

organic matter: decaying plants and animals.

organism: any living thing.

passive solar: use of the sun's energy to heat buildings or water.

photon: a particle of light.

photosynthesis: the process of converting the sun's energy into food in plants.

photovoltaics: technology used to convert sunlight into electricity.

piston: a sliding piece that moves up and down or back and forth.

prediction: what you think will happen.

pump storage: a system for moving water using extra electricity, storing the water, then allowing the water to flow through turbines to create electricity when it's needed.

rays: lines of light that come from a bright object.

reflect: to redirect something that hits a surface, such as heat, light, or sound.

renewable energy: a form of energy that doesn't get used up, including the energy of the sun and the wind.

researcher: a person who systematically studies something.

reservoir: a natural or manmade body of water stored for future use.

retrofit: to change a part or add new parts that were not originally available.

revolution: a human-led dramatic change in something.

runaway greenhouse effect: when a planet's atmosphere gets hotter and hotter, never cooling down, because it has too much heat-trapping greenhouse gases in its atmosphere.

scientific method: the way scientists ask questions and do experiments to try to prove their ideas.

seismic waves: a form of energy released by earthquakes.

smart grid: a computer-based remote control and automated system for electricity delivery. It includes two-way interaction between the generation facilities, utilities, and consumers.

solar cell: a photovoltaic cell that converts sunlight directly into electricity.

solar panel: a device used to capture sunlight and convert it to usable energy.

solar power: energy from the sun converted to electricity.

solar thermal: technology used to heat water from the sun and convert it into electricity.

species: a group of living things that are closely related and produce young.

STEM: stands for science, technology, engineering, and math.

survey: to examine or measure something.

sustainable: a process or resource that can be used without being completely used up or destroyed.

technology: tools, methods, and systems used to solve a problem or do work.

thermal: energy in the form of heat.

topsoil: the top layer of soil.

trade-off: a compromise.

turbine: a device that uses pressure on blades by water, air, or steam to spin generators and create electricity.

urea: a waste product made by animal cells.

water cycle: the movement of water from land to bodies of water, into the atmosphere, and back to the earth.

water vapor: the gaseous form of water in the air.

wind farm: groups or clusters of wind turbines that produce large amounts of electricity together.

windmill: a machine rotated by wind to pump water or do work.

Metric Conversions

Use this chart to find the metric equivalents to the English measurements in this book. If you need to know a half measurement, divide by two. If you need to know twice the measurement, multiply by two. How do you find a quarter measurement? How do you find three times the measurement?

English	Metric
1 inch	2.5 centimeters
1 foot	30.5 centimeters
1 yard	0.9 meter
1 mile	1.6 kilometers
1 pound	0.5 kilogram
1 teaspoon	5 milliliters
1 tablespoon	15 milliliters
1 cup	237 milliliters

WEBSITES

Office of Energy Efficiency and Renewable Energy: *energy.gov/education*
Find videos, lessons, and activities about energy.

National Energy Education Development Project: *need.org*
Offers lesson plans, projects, and education about energy.

My Energy Gateway: *myenergygateway.org*
Find information on degrees and certifications in energy industries,
including information on tuition, scholarships, internships, college
rankings, career options, and industry resources.

The Green Education Foundation: *greeneducationfoundation.org*
A nonprofit organization that provides curriculum and resources to K-12 students
and teachers worldwide with the goal of challenging youth to think holistically and
critically about global environmental, social, and economic concerns and solutions.

Alliance to Save Energy: *ase.org*
A nonprofit organization that promotes energy efficiency
worldwide through research, education and advocacy.

"What You Need To Know about Energy": *needtoknow.nas.edu/energy*
This interactive website from the National Academies of Sciences, Engineering,
and Medicine is a reliable source for information and science related to energy.

The National Academies YouTube channel: *youtube.com/user/nationalacademies*
A great resource for energy and climate change videos.

Science360 Knowledge Network: *science360.gov*
This website gathers the latest science videos provided by scientists,
colleges and universities, science and engineering centers, the National
Science Foundation, and more. A search of "energy" on the site yields
some great short and long videos on a wide range of topics.

U.S. Energy Information Administration - Energy for Kids: *eia.gov/kids*
Offers relevant games and good information.

U.S. Department of Energy - Energy 101 Videos: *energy.gov/videos*
A general video site that can be searched for other topics and energy-related talks.

U.S. Department of Energy - Energy Saver: *energy.gov/energysaver/energy-saver*
Beyond providing information about low-cost ways to lower household energy
bills, the site also provides information about local tax credits, rebates, and
energy-efficiency financing that might be available in different communities.

RESOURCES

QR CODE INDEX

ESSENTIAL QUESTIONS

Introduction: *Why is renewable energy considered a clean energy?*

Chapter 1: *How can we use the sun to produce energy here on the earth?*

Chapter 2: *Why do we think of wind as another form of solar energy?*

Chapter 3: *What methods can we use to harness the power of moving water?*

Chapter 4: *What is geothermal energy and how can we make it useful?*

Chapter 5: *Why does biofuel make sense as an alternative to gasoline?*

Chapter 6: *Which renewable energy is the best choice for these different uses: fueling cars, heating homes, producing electricity, warming water, and powering factories?*

To my amazing wife—thank you for everything you do.
To my three beautiful girls—as Oscar Wilde said so well, "Be yourself;
everyone else is already taken."

—Joshua Sneideman

To my sister, Morgan Twamley, and our future planet.

—Erin Twamley

~ Other Nomad Press Titles Related to Renewable Energy ~

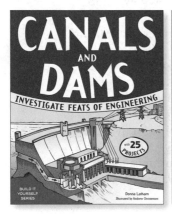
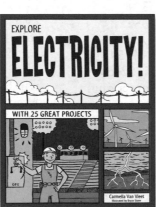

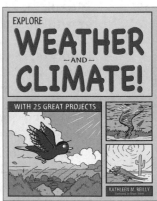

Check out more titles at www.nomadpress.net